# Digital Publis~~~
# Adobe® InDesign® CS6

D0117280

## Sandee Cohen
## Diane Burns

Adobe

**Digital Publishing with Adobe® InDesign® CS 6**

**Sandee Cohen and Diane Burns**

Adobe Press books are published by:

Peachpit
1249 Eighth Street
Berkeley, CA 94710

Peachpit is a division of Pearson Education.

For the latest on Adobe Press books, go to www.adobepress.com.

To report errors, please send a note to errata@peachpit.com

Copyright © 2013 by Sandee Cohen and Diane Burns

Adobe Press Editor: Victor Gavenda
Editor: Becky Morgan
Development Editor: Bob Lindstrom
Production Editor: Becky Winter
Copyeditor: Scout Festa
Indexer: Valerie Haynes Perry
Cover design: Mimi Heft
Interior design: Sandee Cohen and Diane Burns

## Notice of Rights

All rights reserved. No part of this book may be reproduced or transmitted in any form by any means, electronic, mechanical, photocopying, recording, or otherwise, without the prior written permission of the publisher. For information on getting permission for reprints and excerpts, contact permissions@peachpit. com.

## Notice of Liability

The information in this book is distributed on an "As Is" basis, without warranty. While every precaution has been taken in the preparation of the book, neither the authors, Adobe Systems, Inc., nor the publisher shall have any liability to any person or entity with respect to any loss or damage caused or alleged to be caused directly or indirectly by the instructions contained in this book or by the computer software and hardware products described in it.

## Trademarks

Adobe, Adobe Digital Publishing Suite, and InDesign are either registered trademarks or trademarks of Adobe Systems Incorporated in the United States and/or other countries.
All other trademarks are the property of their respective owners.

Many of the designations used by manufacturers and sellers to distinguish their products are claimed as trademarks. Where those designations appear in this book, and Peachpit was aware of a trademark claim, the designations appear as requested by the owner of the trademark. All other product names and services identified throughout this book are used in editorial fashion only and for the benefit of such companies with no intention of infringement of the trademark. No such use, or the use of any trade name, is intended to convey endorsement or other affiliation with this book.

ISBN-13: 978-0-321-82373-1
ISBN-10: 0-321-82373-7

9 8 7 6 5 4 3 2 1

Printed and bound in the United States of America

# Our Thanks To

**Becky Morgan**, our Peachpit editor; **Bob Lindstrom**, the development editor; **Scout Festa**, our copy editor; **Becky Winter**, our production editor; **Liz Welch**, our proofreader, **Valerie Haynes Perry**, our indexer; **Mimi Heft**, the cover designer, and **Nancy Ruenzel**, the publisher of Peachpit Press.

**Victor Gavenda** of Adobe Press for helping guide the initial development of the book.

**Chris Kitchener, Kiyomasa Toma, Annemarie Belliard**, and **Colin Fleming** of Adobe Systems for answering our questions about the intricacies and fast-moving developments of digital publishing from InDesign.

**Gabe Harbs** of In-Tools for his support in allowing us use of the Side-Heads plug-in. http://www.in-tools.com/

**Steve Werner** for his contribution to the ePub and HTML chapter.

**Bob Levine** for his guidance on working with ePub and HTML.

**Anne-Marie Concepcion** for her emergency answers to ePub questions.

**Robert Shaw** of Weldon Owen for use of images.

**Denise Lever** of TransPacific Digital for design support.

From Sandee    **Terry DuPrât** for her support during the deadlines. **Cini**, my Russian Blue cat. And my co-author, **Diane Burns**, without whom I could not have done this book.

From Diane    Ditto on the co-author thing, **Sandee Cohen**.

# Colophon

This book was created using a 13" MacBook Pro, a 15" MacBook Pro and a 27" iMac. Windows screen shots were taken on a Dell Vostro.

Pages were laid out using Adobe InDesign CS 5.5. Illustrations were created using Adobe Photoshop CS 5 and Adobe Illustrator CS 5. Fonts used were Chaparral Pro and Gill Sans Std.

Screen shots were taken using SnapzPro (Mac) and Snagit (Win).

The automatic positioning of anchored side heads was created using the Side Heads plug-in from in-tools (in-tools.com).

The word cloud illustrations at the front of each chapter were created using the Wordalizer script from indiscripts (indiscripts.com).

Weekly video conferences were held using iChat.

Files were shared using Dropbox Pro.

# Table of Contents

# Introduction

# In This Chapter

THE LAST TIME TECHNOLOGY WAS SO DISRUPTIVE to the field of graphic design and publishing was back in the 1980s, when page layout programs were part of a revolution called desktop publishing. Designers and publishers could use programs such as PageMaker or QuarkXPress to set type right at their desks—hence the term desktop publishing.

Designers had to learn new skills—not just to design pages and art, but to make documents flow correctly and import images with the correct color space and resolution. They had to deal with digital typefaces and missing fonts. (Fonts were *always* missing!)

But for the longest time, those programs stayed basically the same. Their final output was geared to print publishing. New features were added, but they were always for the printed page.

Slowly, though, the publishing landscape began to change. File formats from Photoshop included the GIF and JPEG images used for web pages. A new page layout program called InDesign leveraged Adobe's PDF format to create PDF documents that could be posted and read on the web. Slowly, print designers were exposed to new concepts in computer graphics, mostly related to the web and onscreen PDFs. Designers had to learn a new set of skills for digital and interactive document production.

But all that change was tame compared to what has happened in the past three to four years. The number of print books sold has been surpassed by the number of books downloaded from sites such as Amazon and iTunes. Print magazines have been brought back to life as interactive applications. Corporations are creating presentations for computer screens instead of printed brochures.

It's a whole new world of digital publishing. Exciting times, yes, but the print designer has to rethink and relearn a whole new world.

# Who Are We?

We both have backgrounds in traditional publishing, including advertising and design. But individually we have worked with clients to help them create interactive PDF presentations, ePubs, and tablet applications. We've added movies and interactive elements to educational materials that were originally created for print output, and posted them online. Both of us have taught hundreds of hours of classes on the new digital output formats. We've written articles and books on how to create interactive

PDF documents. And the two of us have seen our own print books sold as ePubs on Amazon and iTunes.

**It hasn't been easy** That's not to say we haven't struggled. Both of us had to learn how to format media files so they work on multiple output devices. We had to learn how to read basic HTML and CSS code and learn the proper formats in which to hand over our projects to web designers and Flash ActionScript developers. Both of us had to learn how to apply and modify animation controls. And most of all, we had to learn how to think differently about the presentation of information that's in a digital format, free from the printed page.

So we feel much empathy with you. That's why we wrote this book. This is the book that we wish we'd had years ago to take us through the intricacies of digital publishing.

# Who Are You?

You are the students we've taught for the past few years who are struggling to keep up with the new technologies. You might be a designer who suddenly realizes that you need to master the features of complicated and strange workflows. You could be a department head who is looking to expand from print into digital production and needs to know the right format for each job. You're a freelancer who needs to improve your skills to keep up with the latest trends.

Most likely you're confused and overwhelmed. This book was written with you in mind.

Don't feel alone. This sea change affects every designer, publisher, and creative professional in every field. The following sections outline the impact on those in many different roles.

**Advertising designers** Advertising has been at the forefront of creating ads and marketing information for digital publications. For instance, interactive 360° images can be used to show a car interior, and panoramas can show the beautiful vistas seen from the newest resort hotel. Videos can show any product in a way that print never could.

Today's advertising art directors and creative directors need to understand the possibilities for converting the layouts for print ads and brochures into digital publications. They need to know how to convert television commercials into videos that can be incorporated into digital delivery. They will want to change an ad's orientation from horizontal to vertical — while perhaps changing its content as well.

This ad for MasterCard takes advantage of the dual orientation for tablets. It shows certain information in the vertical orientation (left) and different information in the horizontal view (right).

**Book designers**

It's hard to find a major (or minor) publishing house that is not creating ePubs. Their challenge is to maintain design standards within the limited layout controls of the ePub formats but at the same time understand what enhancements can be made to eBooks. And they need to evaluate what new workflow and staff are necessary to manage both print and digital publishing.

The broad distribution of ePubs has added new life to old books.

**Magazine designers**

Many major magazine publishers have enthusiastically embraced converting their magazines into digital publications. Their designers have been leaders in using InDesign's Digital Publishing Suite (DPS) for designing interactive apps to achieve exciting results.

*Wired* was the very first magazine to use InDesign and DPS tools to create an app for the iPad. With help from Adobe, that first issue became a landmark publication, with almost every interactive technique featured in the magazine. Since then, *Wired* has continued to make their digital publication as cutting-edge as possible.

*Wired* magazine has used videos in its digital version. In this example, an article on spies features a video of the opening of the James Bond movies.

Magazines have even created content for their digital versions that doesn't appear in the print version. For instance, *People* magazine's digital version has a final page feature that shows different covers from the past 35 years.

An example of the special feature on cover images that appears in the digital — but not the print — edition of *People* magazine.

In addition, magazine publishers have created new subscription options. Many print subscriptions now also include access to the digital version. Condé Nast, Hearst, Meredith, News Corp., and Time Inc. have created a new subscription model called Next Issue. Sometimes referred to as "Netflix for magazines," it allows, for a monthly fee, unlimited access to the publishers' entire catalog of magazines.

**In-house marketing designers**

We've worked with many marketing departments who long ago embraced digital publications. Even if it was just a simple PDF of a print brochure, they were already using digital delivery for their sales message. They also were pleased with the relatively small cost of digital distribution compared to that of print runs with shipping and mailing costs.

Then they discovered how the features of interactive displays, video, and form fields could further enhance their PDFs. Today these designers are looking to interactive PDF as well as adding new digital formats to their marketing programs.

Instead of having a printed brochure mailed to them, Cunard customers can instantly download a PDF brochure.

**Clients**

Many clients are asking their design firms or ad agencies to "put something on the iPad." That sort of vague direction doesn't target the right audience for their product. In fact, there are many different types of files that can be delivered via tablet devices, including those we discuss in this book: interactive PDF, ePub, tablet app, and HTML. So a vague direction is no good at all.

The best clients are those who understand the possibilities (and limitations) of digital publications. They understand which format does what. And they understand that a certain format may be better for their needs. More than ever, today's designers need to educate their clients about what options make sense for them.

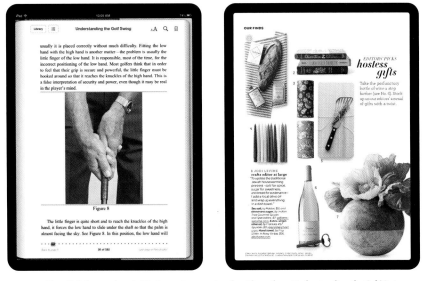

The ePub format is suitable for an instructional guide such as *Understanding the Golf Swing* (left). But a catalog or magazine, like *Martha Stewart Living* (right), is more effective as a tablet app, where the user can tap each item for more information.

**What you need to know before you use this book**

While you may be a beginner in digital publishing, you shouldn't be a beginner when it comes to creating InDesign documents. We're assuming you have a pretty good knowledge of how to import graphics, format text, and use paragraph styles, object styles, and layers. If you need basic training, we recommend the *InDesign CS6 Visual QuickStart Guide* by Sandee Cohen.

However, we don't expect you to have extensive knowledge of interactive features such as buttons, form fields, hyperlinks, electronic tables of contents, and media. We'll take you through those features completely.

## Print isn't dead!

The rise of digital publishing doesn't mean that there won't still be print books, magazines, and so on. *LensWork* magazine is a good example of how print and digital can work together. The print magazine is a 96-page bimonthly that focuses on photography and the creative process. It uses duotones and high-quality printing to present photographers' portfolios.

*LensWork Extended* is a PDF-based bimonthly multimedia publication containing lots of additional content that simply won't fit in the 96 pages of *LensWork*. It also features color portfolios not seen in the print publication. The magazine has editions formatted specifically for the iPad and for Android tablet devices.

All the formats work together for the benefit of *LensWork* subscribers.

# Digital Publishing Formats

There are many different formats for digital output from InDesign. The following are the digital formats you're most likely to use as you explore the possibilities of digital publishing.

| Format | Description | Benefits/Disadvantages | Chapter |
|---|---|---|---|
| DPS | Interactive applications that can be uploaded onto devices such as the Apple iPad and Android tablets. | Can be sold through the Apple App Store and Google Play. Requires a high degree of skill to create. | 6 |
| ePub | Documents, often long, that can be read on eReaders such as iBooks, Kindle, and Nook. ePubs can also be read on computer screens using eReader software. | Can be sold through Amazon, iBooks, and other online marketplaces. Requires a certain degree of skill to export successfully. | 5 |
| HTML | Code-based text and images that are posted to web pages and viewed on computers or tablets. | Can be passed on to developers to include in websites. Does not create a finished website automatically. | 5 |
| PDF | Page-based documents that can be downloaded from websites or distributed via email or disks. Can be viewed on computers or tablets, but not all features are supported by all readers and devices. | Easily exported with interactive features. No online sales stores. | 7 |
| SWF and FLA | Based on Adobe Flash technology, these formats can be used as interactive presentations containing motion graphics and videos. | Easy to create sophisticated motion graphics without using Flash ActionScript code. Not available on any iOS device. | 7 |

## Why "digital publishing" isn't quite right

We went round and round trying to come up with the right title to describe the techniques and digital formats we cover in this book. "Digital delivery" and "electronic publishing" were just two of the other choices. Our problem was that there really isn't any uniform label that covers the broad range of digital publishing. And if you think about it, any document, even one destined for print output, is "digital" when it's created in InDesign.

When asked by our friends and family what our book was about, we'd give them the title. But then we'd expand on it by saying, "It's about creating the non-print export formats from InDesign."

So despite a title that isn't perfect, if you've read this far, you must have recognized what this book covers and why it's the right book for you.

# InDesign Workflows

InDesign has been, and is, at the center of the print design and production workflow, bringing together text, illustrations, and photographs from other programs. For digital publications, it becomes even more central in the workflow. It assembles information and assets, and its powerful export features and integration with Adobe's Digital Publishing Suite make it more essential than ever — the "hub" of your publishing workflow.

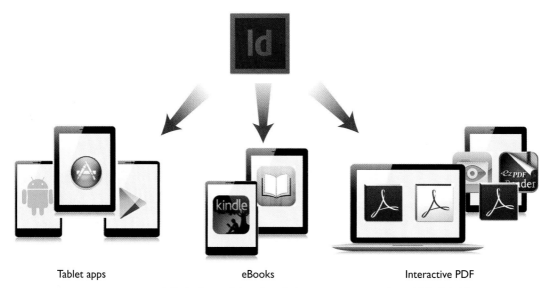

| Tablet apps | eBooks | Interactive PDF |

InDesign is one of the only tools that can create content for multiple digital formats.

**InDesign as the "hub"**

This book is very "InDesign-centric," focusing on InDesign documents as the center of your workflow. Once you have created an InDesign file, it can be exported to a print PDF, an interactive PDF, an eBook, a tablet application, and so on. Corrections, updates, and changes are made to the original InDesign file and then re-exported to the various output formats.

**Focus on InDesign features**

We've had to narrow the scope of the book to cover InDesign's features. For instance, InDesign lets you add interactive buttons and forms to documents for PDF export. While these features are exciting, they do not cover all the functionality found in Acrobat, Adobe's PDF editing software. Rather than dipping into Acrobat, though, we've limited ourselves to just InDesign's features for interactive PDFs.

Similarly, the workflow to create DPS apps and eBooks for the iPad relies on working with Apple to get approval for those products. We mention the process only briefly, as we can't fully cover the requirements of third-party companies, especially those for creating applications.

And we don't focus on some of the very important overall strategies. For example, building responsive websites using HTML5 may turn out to be one of the best and most flexible ways to produce digital content. But InDesign's role in that strategy is quite limited, so we don't cover building websites.

**What is expected of a print designer?** It's likely that when you started as a print designer, you had a basic understanding of the print process. You may have interacted directly with a printing company, making sure your files were set up to print correctly. But you never had to print the job yourself. And you usually were not responsible for the distribution of the printed piece, because that was up to your client or your client's marketing department.

But with digital publishing, there are many different things you may need to know. When a client says, "I want my document on Kindle and iPad," there's a lot more involved in setting up your files correctly. You need to understand much more about how files are distributed and the limitations of each digital format. We'll cover what jobs you need to know how to do and what you can safely ask others to finish.

For instance, many design firms have separate departments for print and web. You may not need to know Cascading Style Sheets (CSS) or Hypertext Markup Language (HTML), but you should know the proper ways to create the InDesign file that you'll hand off to the next team.

This includes creating styles. Styles are essential; not only paragraph and character styles, but also object styles and table and cell styles have become essential in creating digital content. If you aren't up to speed on using styles for print documents, few would know the difference (though you may spend extra hours producing the work), but you can't live without them in the new digital world.

# Thinking Digitally

There are other new skills that you need to use to work with digital publications. Most of all, you need to think differently.

**Planning ahead** It does no good to be halfway through a project only to find out that the videos you were relying on won't play in all formats, or that there's no software to play your document on a certain type of tablet.

These chapters contain many tables that compare which features can be used in each type of digital publication. This can help you choose the right type of format. You'll also find a few "war stories" that illustrate how a lack of planning can cause problems when the product is published.

**Thinking non-linearly** As a print designer, you're used to linear documents. Books start at the front page and work their way to the end. Ads start at the top of the page and read down. But digital publishing allows you to move off in many different directions.

Consider the story "Little Red Riding Hood." While a book may flow from one page to another, a tablet app of the story can have tangents that send the reader to recipes for the goodies in the basket, an article on the wolves of North America, and the medical options for senior citizens.

Digital publications also provide opportunities for non-text features. For "Little Red Riding Hood," this could include interactive maps for the route to Grandma's house, videos of the latest movie about the story, or puzzles and games for children reading the story.

**New ways of thinking about a page**

In print documents, a page has no depth. Images don't hide under each other. There are no layers to turn on to see things below. But in digital publications, a page can be as deep as you want. Images can be stacked one on top of another and be revealed by clicking buttons. The digital publishing designer should learn how to think in this new dimension.

The size of the objects on a page is flexible. Text can scroll into view within a small opening on the page. This makes it possible to present long recipes and other instructional text without taking up a lot of page real estate or reducing the type size. It's a new way to present material on each page.

*Better Homes and Gardens* magazine uses a scrolling area to display more copy than would ordinarily fit on the page.

**Adding multimedia to magazines and books**

Creating digital publications also means that you can use video and audio files to enhance publications. This means you have to own or acquire the rights to use these files. Files also have to be in the proper format.

All of this requires a little extra work, but media files add tremendously to publications. We worked with an author who wrote an ePub guidebook based on his years of taking tourists around Rome. Instead of just describing a certain market or attraction, he inserted videos that show what to look for. The ePub guidebook is selling well—especially considering it was self-published, with little outside marketing.

**Special features**

Some features are automatically added to digital publications. Those who have read eBooks know that there is a built-in dictionary in iBooks and Kindle devices. Readers can look up the definition of any word they don't know, and the definition is displayed right on the eBook page.

Readers can also highlight text, add notes, and search within text. This definitely enhances the process of reading. And the designer doesn't have to do a thing to make it happen.

An eBook page in iBooks with a highlight, a note, and the definition of a selected word.

**Engaging the reader**

One important thing about advertising, especially direct mail, is that the longer someone engages with your material, the more likely they are to buy the product. Adding interactivity and multimedia to digital content, including advertising, helps keep the reader engaged. The longer someone plays with the buttons, watches movies, and works with elements on the page, the more positive feelings they will have toward the content or product.

**Educating the reader**

While it's not necessary to show readers of print books how to turn a page, you do need to educate your audience on how to use the interactive and media features in your document. This may include an opening screen with instructions for the icons and features in your document. It may also include text and icons on the pages that alert the reader to an interactive feature.

A page of instructions appears at the top of the digital version of *Better Homes and Gardens*.

As readers become more familiar with the conventions used in digital publications, these types of instructions will become less necessary. Of course, as the next generation of readers comes of age, they will be far more comfortable using screens for digital publications. We're reminded of a YouTube video that shows a 1-year-old expertly using an iPad — pinching and swiping — and then trying the same moves on a paper magazine without results.

## Don't let the media drive the design

We've seen interactivity used just for the sake of interaction. For instance, one of the DPS magazine apps we've looked at has photos that require you to click a button to view the photo caption. There is plenty of room on the page for the caption. And clicking the button is actually more work for the reader. But the designer of the app wanted to have the reader play with a button rather than just see the image and read the caption. That's when your digital publication becomes a fad, not communication.

# Keeping Up With It All

Unlike print production technology, the digital publishing standards that are in effect when you start a project may change by the time you're done, and the content you created and want to maintain and distribute may be rendered obsolete. Apple may change the process to upload apps or ePubs. Adobe may release new versions of the DPS tools. New PDF readers may become available for the iPad and other tablets. Amazon or Apple may change the features in their Kindle or iBooks publications.

You also may need to buy and maintain different hardware devices and software so you can test to make sure your digital publications run properly on each device. This includes computers running different operating systems; various versions of the iPad; and different versions of Android tablets, Amazon Kindles, and Barnes & Noble Nooks. In fact, you will most likely be designing for devices that haven't been invented yet.

If it seems confusing, part of the reason is that digital publishing is in its very early stages and it's a bit like the wild, wild West out there.

When we first started writing this book, we tried to make a diagram that clearly showed which InDesign interactive features could be output in each format. We soon ended up splitting the diagram into different devices, different manufacturers, and different reader apps to the point that it became more confusing than helpful. As of this writing, for example, video in an ePub doesn't play on a branded Kindle reader, but it will play when viewed by Kindle reader software on a laptop or iPad. Or take buttons in PDFs: They work great when viewed on a computer, but when it comes to the iPad, different reader apps have different capabilities — buttons work in PDF Expert on the iPad but not in Adobe Reader on the iPad. And on it goes.

Digital publishing is as disruptive a technology to designers and publishers as desktop publishing was back in the 1980s. Standards are yet to be set; temporary players in the market have yet to be winnowed out. But still, you have to start somewhere. We hope that you'll find this book an ideal starting point.

As for the wild West out there, you'll find additional resources listed in several of the chapters. And because digital publishing is rapidly changing, we're going to continue to help you keep current with new information on our blog.

---

**TIP** Visit our blog at www.indesigndigitalpublishing.com. We'll add information on new features and on new processes for creating digital publications as it becomes available. You can also email us at info@indesigndigitalpublishing.com with any questions or comments you may have. We'd love to hear from you.

---

# Interactive Tools

# In This Chapter

IMAGINE THAT HENRY LUCE, THE MAN WHO CREATED *TIME*, *LIFE*, AND *SPORTS ILLUSTRATED* MAGAZINES, were to come from the past to visit you today. What would you show him to get him excited about the power of digital publications?

Well, you'd start by showing him how each digital publication could have hyperlinks and buttons that allow the reader to click one page and instantly jump to another. You'd definitely want to play movies and sounds that enhance the printed text. You might even have him fill out an electronic subscription application that could be instantly transmitted back to Time/Life magazines.

This chapter is all about creating the interactive tools that give digital publications the figurative—and literal—bells and whistles that make them so exciting to view.

# Types of Interactive Elements

There are nine types of interactive elements you can add to InDesign documents: hyperlinks, cross-references, bookmarks, audio/video files, multi-state objects, buttons, forms, animations, and page transitions. Each has its own particular uses, but some of the features may overlap. Before you start work, you need to decide which type of interactive element is right for your job or you could be stuck with an effect that can't be exported for your finished project.

| Feature | What It Does | How Used | Limitations | Available for |
|---|---|---|---|---|
| Hyperlinks | Adds a hotspot area to text or objects where you can click to move to other parts of the document, other documents, or web pages. Can also be used to send email documents. | Can be applied directly to the text inside a story. Hyperlinks can also be automatically applied to the entries in a table of contents or index using those InDesign features. | Provides only very primitive visual indications of the linked area. | ePubs DPS apps PDF SWF (Not all Link To options are supported in ePubs and DPS apps.) |
| Cross-References | Adds a hotspot area to text that is linked to other parts of the document. | Also adds dynamic text that indicates the position of the cross-reference. | Provides only primitive visual indications of the linked area. | ePubs DPS apps PDF |

| Feature | What It Does | How Used | Limitations | Available for |
|---|---|---|---|---|
| Table of Contents | Creates a list of all the paragraphs that contain certain paragraph styles along with the page numbers for those paragraphs. The list for each paragraph is a type of hyperlink to the referenced page. | Used to create navigational elements in a PDF. | Requires the use of paragraph styles for text. | PDF |
| Bookmarks | Adds a navigational element that is visible in the Bookmarks pane of Adobe Reader or Adobe Acrobat. | The Bookmark pane can be set to be visible at all times in the PDF document. Can be created automatically using the Table of Contents feature. | Requires some education to teach the reader how to use the Bookmarks pane in the Reader. Is not directly on the document page. No special visual indication in the document. | PDF |
| Audio or Video Files | Adds sounds or video files that can be played in exported documents. | Adds descriptive elements to the finished file. Can be prompted by buttons. | Adds to the size of the exported file. | PDF ePubs (Not all eReaders support playing audio or video elements.) DPS apps SWF |
| Multi-State Objects | Creates a single element that can display different items. | Can create slideshows or other displays of elements on a page. Interactive elements such as buttons and movies can also be made part of a multi-state object. | Can be exported only for DPS applications. | DPS apps |

| Feature | What It Does | How Used | Limitations | Available for |
|---|---|---|---|---|
| Buttons | Adds a hotspot area that can contain text or graphics. This hotspot can be set to invoke a wide variety of behaviors, including navigation as well as movie or audio playback. | Offers the most navigational and design choices. | Buttons can't be created automatically from text or styles. Requires the most work to create. | DPS apps PDF SWF |
| Forms | Adds an area that can be used in Acrobat to enter information or to mark check boxes or radio buttons. | These forms can be filled out in the PDF and the information then sent back to the creator for tabulation. | Forms can't be created automatically. Requires the most work to create. | PDF |
| Animations (*covered in Chapter 3, "Animations"*) | Applies motions to page elements that can be displayed as part of a SWF video. | Easier to learn and use than Adobe Flash Pro. | Can be used only in SWF exports. | SWF |
| Page Transitions (*covered in Chapter 7, "Exporting PDF and SWF"*) | Creates an effect, such as a dissolve, when you move from one page to another. | Easy to apply. | The Page Turn and Page Curl effects are available only for SWF export. | PDF SWF |

# Defining Hyperlinks

A hyperlink is an area of a page that can be clicked to send the reader to a new page, open a new document, move to a web page, or send an email message. There are two parts to a hyperlink: The *source* is the object or text that is clicked to trigger the hyperlink; the *destination* is the page, web link, or action that you go to.

Creating a hyperlink

If the Hyperlinks panel is not visible, choose Window > Interactive > Hyperlinks to open the panel. In addition to the panel menu, there are buttons at the bottom of the panel that control many of the hyperlink and cross-reference functions.

The Hyperlinks panel is where you choose new hyperlinks.

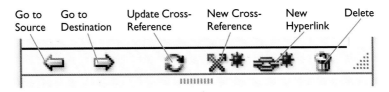

The buttons at the bottom of the Hyperlinks panel control many of the functions for creating hyperlinks and cross-references.

Select the text or object that you want to make the hyperlink source. (New Hyperlink isn't available unless text or an object is selected.) Click the **New Hyperlink** button in the panel or choose **New Hyperlink** from the panel menu. This opens the New Hyperlink dialog box.

The New Hyperlink dialog box is where you set the type of link, destination, character style, and appearance for a hyperlink.

Set the options for **Link To**, **Destination**, **Character Style**, and **Appearance** as described in the following sections.

Setting the Link To and
Destination options

There are three types of destinations for hyperlinks. You can link to a specific place in a document, open a web page or file, or send an email. The type of destination you choose determines the options that appear in the New Hyperlink dialog box.

As you create hyperlinks, be aware that some of the destinations or attributes do not work in all media, but you can rely on all these features to work in PDF or SWF files. For instance, a PDF or SWF file may support opening another type of file or simply going to another page in the document. But those types of destinations may be deleted completely when you export to an ePub or DPS application. And even then there may not be any consistency among the various eBook reader software.

An email destination works just fine in the iBooks software on an iPad, but it is deleted entirely on the original Kindle. So a destination that works for iBooks may not work for Kindle or Nook software. We know it's expensive to keep up with all the new tablets and eReaders, but in order to truly rely on certain links, you must test them on the physical devices your readers are going to be using.

Here are the types of hyperlink destinations found in the Link To menu:
URL: Choose this to enter a universal resource locator (URL) as the destination. This needs to be a complete URL, such as http://www.adobe.com. You can also use any of the other protocols, such as http://, file://, ftp://, or mailto://.

TIP If you have an extremely long URL, it may not work correctly. In that case you can use one of the URL shortening services, such as bit.ly, tinyURL.com, or goo.gl.

When you choose URL as the Link To option, the Destination area gives you a URL field where you can enter the address for the web page you want the hyperlink to go to.

File: This creates a link that opens a file in another application. This is used for PDF documents, which can then open a file such as another PDF, a word-processing file, or a spreadsheet document. It is not used in ePubs or DPS applications.

When you create a destination to open a file, you need to enter the absolute path for the file. This is the complete route from the hard drive down to the directory that contains the file. This is so that Acrobat knows where the file is located. A relative path, with just the name of the file, won't work, even if the file is located in the same folder as the PDF document. In addition, the person who clicks the link must have the appropriate software to open the linked file.

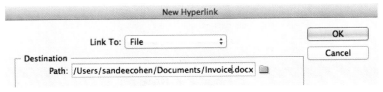

When you choose File as the Link To option, the Destination area gives you a Path field where you can enter the path where the file is located. You can also click the folder icon to navigate to the file.

Email: This option creates a link that opens the default email application on the user's computer. Use the **Address field** to enter the email address, such as user@domain.com. Use the **Subject Line field** to enter a subject for the message. This type of destination relies on the software on the reading device. A Kindle doesn't have any email software, so the link to open an email application doesn't do anything on a Kindle. But iPads and other tablets do have mail programs, so clicking the email link will prompt a new email.

When you choose Email as the Link To option, the Destination area gives you an Address field where you can enter the email address. The Subject Line field lets you enter a subject for the message.

Page: This creates a link that opens a new page in the current document or a different document. You have the option to choose an open document or browse to select another document. This type of hyperlink is not used in ePub or DPS applications. Those documents have no idea of pages, so they discard the information for a page link.

You might hesitate to apply a page link if you expect to add or delete pages to the document so that the page you designated as the destination moves to a different position. That's actually not a problem. The hyperlink is tied to the actual page, not the page number. So if you have a link from page one to page three and you add two pages after page one, the link will then take you to page five.

However, the opposite situation happens if you add two pages of text to a story so that the text that was on page three moves to page five. In that case, the hyperlink continues to take you to page three, which no longer contains the same text. In order to ensure that the link always goes to a specific point in the text, you need to link to a text anchor.

When you choose Page as the Link To option, the Destination area displays the options for document, pages, and zoom setting.

**Text Anchor:** This creates a link to a point in the text that was previously defined as a text anchor. The text anchor can be in the same document or a different document. This is the only type of destination that needs to be created before you define the source link. (*See the section on page 28 to learn how to create text anchors.*) We have gotten excellent results using text anchor links in ePubs.

TIP The difference between a Page link and a Text Anchor link is that the Page link uses the entire page as the destination. The Text Anchor link allows you to focus on a specific position on the page.

When you choose Text Anchor as the Link To option, the Destination area lets you choose a document as well as a previously created text anchor.

**Shared Destination:** This creates a link to a previously defined hyperlink. This is particularly helpful if you want several different hyperlinks to go to the same destination.

New Hyperlink

Link To: Shared Destination

OK

Cancel

Destination
Document: The Old Man and the Sea study.indd
Name: http://www.studyingernest.com
URL (http://www.studyingernest.com)

When you choose Shared Destination as the Link To option, the Destination area gives you a Document menu where you can choose the document that contains the shared link. The Name menu contains all the shared destinations for that document.

**Viewing the icons in the Hyperlinks panel**

As you define hyperlinks, they appear in the Hyperlinks panel. Each type of hyperlink displays a different icon.

Chittenango, New York    URL or Email link

goes into the oil business and becom    Text Anchor link

quick bio    Page link

The icon next to each hyperlink tells you the type of destination for that link.

TIP A selected hyperlink also displays its URL or other link information in the Hyperlinks panel.

As you work, you may need to change the name of a hyperlink in the panel. Whereas most listings in panels can be renamed by simply double-clicking the entry, to rename a hyperlink you need to choose the **Rename Hyperlink** command from the Hyperlinks panel menu.

**Setting the style and appearance of hyperlinks**

In addition to setting the destinations for hyperlinks, you can control how a hyperlink appears in the exported document. These settings are almost always ignored by the software in ePub readers. Each eReader software has its own display for hyperlinks. However, these options translate perfectly to PDF and SWF files.

Setting a character style for hyperlinks

Select the text that you want as a hyperlink. In the New Hyperlink dialog box, click the **Character Style** menu.

Choose a predefined character style, or choose **None** to apply no character style to the selected text.

Character Style
☑ Style: hyperlinks

The Character Style menu lets you apply a character style to the text of a hyperlink.

You can apply a character style to format the text with a special color or underline. But remember, most eBook readers will substitute their own formatting (similar to the appearance of links in a web browser). For instance, you might get the custom color you apply, but the eBook reader may add an underline in a different color.

TIP Character styles are not available when an object is selected as a hyperlink.

### Setting the appearance of a hyperlink

You can also create visual indicators around hyperlinks. This is controlled using the Appearance settings.

The Appearance controls let you apply formatting to the hyperlink in the exported document.

Use the **Type** menu in the Appearance area to choose a setting for the visibility of the rectangle around the hotspot. **Invisible Rectangle** hides the rectangle around the link; **Visible Rectangle** displays a rectangle around the link.

Use the **Width, Style**, and **Color** menus to format the rectangle around the link. We recommend either using a Thin width or, better yet, simply using Invisible Rectangle, as any rectangle style tends to look rather clunky.

Use the **Highlight** menu to choose the appearance of the hotspot area when clicked. **None** applies no change to the look of the area when clicked. **Invert** changes the colors in the area to their inverted RGB colors—black becomes white, white becomes black, red becomes green, and so on. **Outline** draws a rectangle around the area. **Inset** creates the appearance of the area being pushed into the page. These effects are not very sophisticated, and we recommend using them sparingly.

TIP The width of the rectangle stays constant even if the viewer zooms in or out on a PDF page.

To use the Style menu: Choose a solid or dashed line for the visible rectangle. Solid is fine. Dashed is clunky and ugly—we never use it!

To use the Color menu: You can choose one of the colors for a visible rectangle. These colors are not from the Swatches panel.

Editing the source settings

As you work, you can edit the settings for the text area or object that has the hyperlink applied. Double-click the hyperlink entry in the Hyperlinks panel, or select the hyperlink in the Hyperlinks panel and choose Hyperlink Options in the Hyperlinks panel menu. This opens the Hyperlink Options dialog box, which contains all the options of the New Hyperlink dialog box. Make whatever changes you want.

To delete a hyperlink: Select the hyperlink you wish to delete. Click the **Delete** button in the Hyperlinks panel, or choose **Delete Hyperlink/Cross-Reference** from the Hyperlinks panel menu.

TIP Deleting a hyperlink does not delete any character style that was applied to the text. You need to highlight the text and remove the character style using the Character Styles panel.

Creating page destinations without sources

The easiest way to create a hyperlink destination is to create it as you define the hyperlink. However, it's also possible to define destinations without defining the hyperlink source at the same time. This is helpful if you have a lot of destinations that you want to define but don't know where you will apply them. For instance, it may be helpful to create a destination for a company's website before actually applying it within the text.

TIP Destinations don't appear in the Hyperlinks panel. You can see the destinations for a document when you define a new hyperlink.

Choose New Hyperlink Destination in the Hyperlinks panel menu. The New Hyperlink Destination dialog box appears. Choose **Text Anchor**, **Page**, or **URL** from the Type menu. (The File and Email options are available only by typing in the URL.)

The New Hyperlink Destination dialog box lets you define hyperlink destinations without first selecting a source object or text.

Creating a text anchor destination: This is the only type of destination that must be defined here before you create the source hyperlink. Select the text, or place your insertion point at the position where you want the text anchor to be located. Then open the New Hyperlink Destination dialog box and choose Text Anchor from the Type menu.

Use the Name field to name the destination. The text anchor indicator appears in the selected text.

The options for a Text Anchor hyperlink destination.

Creating a URL destination: This is the same as creating a URL destination in the New Hyperlink dialog box, which is covered on page 23.

Creating a Page destination: This is the same as creating a Page destination in the New Hyperlink dialog box, as covered on page 24.

Editing hyperlink destination options

Choose Hyperlink Destination Options from the Hyperlinks panel menu. This is the only place in the document where you can see a list of all the destinations. Select a destination, and click **Edit** to change the name, the link, or other features. These are the same options you had when you first created the destination.

TIP Editing the hyperlink destination doesn't change the appearance of the link. That needs to be modified using the Edit Hyperlink dialog box.

| Hyperlink Destination Options | |
|---|---|
| Destination: InDesign product page | OK |
| Type: URL | Cancel |
| Name: InDesign product page | Edit |
| URL: http://www.adobe.com/produc | Delete |

Choose Hyperlink Destination Options to edit existing destinations.

Navigating through hyperlinks in the document

As you create hyperlinks, you can test to see if they are working correctly by using the controls in the Hyperlinks panel.

To move to a hyperlink: Select the hyperlink in the Hyperlinks panel. Choose Go to Source from the Hyperlinks panel menu, or click the Go to Source button in the Hyperlinks panel.

To move to a hyperlink destination: Select the hyperlink in the Hyperlinks panel. Choose **Go to Destination** from the Hyperlinks panel menu or click the **Go to Destination** button in the Hyperlinks panel.

TIP If the destination is a URL, the default web browser will be launched.

To fix a missing hyperlink: If you have document, page, or text anchor hyperlink destinations, those links may become missing if the document is changed or moved. The hyperlink will then display a missing destination icon: A red circle means the document hyperlink is missing; a red flag means the page or text anchor hyperlink is missing. You then need to re-establish the hyperlink.

Choose Hyperlink Options from the panel menu, or double-click the hyperlink to open the Edit Hyperlink dialog box. (Ignore the alert dialog box that says the hyperlink is missing. You know it's missing.) Set the new destination for the hyperlink. The hyperlink is now fixed.

| Hyperlink | ❷ |
|---|---|
| adf | ▣ |

The missing destination icons in the Hyperlinks panel.

Viewing hyperlinks in the Story Editor

If you don't apply any appearance settings or character styles to hyperlinks, you may not be aware of where they are in the text. One of the best ways to view the location of a hyperlink source is to view your text in the Story Editor. The Story Editor displays a special character for hyperlinks and makes them easy to find in the text.

To access the Story Editor, choose Edit > Story Editor or use the keyboard shortcut Cmd/Ctrl-Y. The Story Editor will open in a separate window. The text in the Story Editor is dynamic, and any changes made in the Story Editor will be reflected immediately in your layout.

TIP Type Cmd/Ctrl-Y again to jump back to the layout at the same position that you were in the Story Editor.

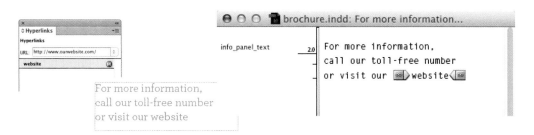

The Story Editor displays special markers for hyperlink sources that make them easy to spot.

You can use the Story Editor to locate hyperlinks and make sure they are applied to the correct text. The Story Editor also displays special characters for hyperlink destinations, cross-references, and text anchors.

# Creating Cross-References

Cross-references are a subset of hyperlinks and are found at the bottom of the Hyperlinks panel. Like hyperlinks, cross-references create an electronic link from one part of a document to a destination in the same document or in a different document. But cross-references do more than hyperlinks do. They are dynamic and can pick up text and information from the destination and include it in the source text. So you can create a cross-reference that says "for more information, see page ###." The page number then updates if the document is modified.

TIP In addition to using cross-references to create links in digital publications, you can use cross-references when creating long print documents. We used them everywhere you see a reference to another page in this book. Without cross-references, we would have had to manually enter the correct page numbers.

## Cross-References in ePubs

Because ePubs have no concept of pages, there's no need to use cross-references to insert dynamic page numbers in text. But that doesn't mean you won't want to use cross-references in ePubs.

A cross-reference can insert text from the destination paragraph or text anchor. This allows you to refer to text elsewhere in the book. For instance, you could have a cross-reference that says "for more information, see the chapter 'Looking at Birds.'" Then, if the chapter title changes to "Bird Watching," the cross-reference changes accordingly.

Also, using the cross-reference feature creates an electronic link within the ePub document. This allows your readers to click to go from one place to another.

**Setting a cross-reference**

Place your insertion point in the text where you want the cross-reference to appear. Unlike hyperlinks, cross-references can be inserted only into text. You can't use an object as the source for a cross-reference.

Click the **New Cross-Reference** icon in the Hyperlinks panel. This opens the New Cross-Reference dialog box. Set the options as described in the following sections.

**Setting the cross-reference Link To options**

Like hyperlinks, cross-references let you point to a destination that you want to link to. However, the links for cross-references are to a specific position in the text. They can also pick up the page number or paragraph content in the linked text. Use the **Link To** menu to choose which type of cross-reference you want. The options are to a text anchor or to a paragraph with a specific paragraph style applied.

**TIP** As with the Text Anchor option for hyperlinks, you need to create a text anchor before you open the New Cross-Reference dialog box.

The New Cross-Reference dialog box lets you set the destination, format, and appearance of a cross-reference.

Setting a text anchor cross-reference

When you choose a text anchor for a cross-reference, the dialog box displays the options for the document and all the text anchors in that document. You need to have previously defined the text anchor for it to appear in that list.

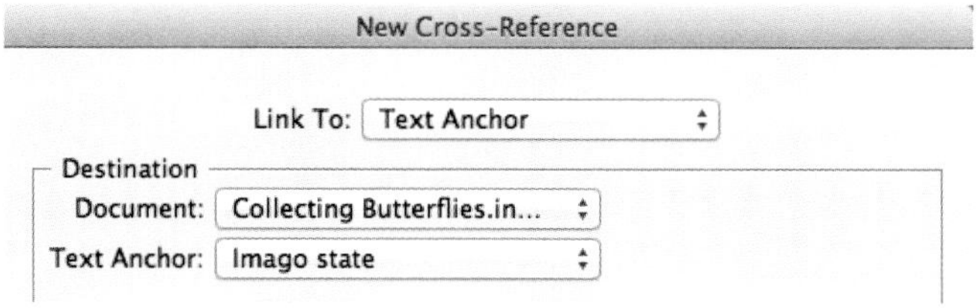

**New Cross-Reference**

Link To: Text Anchor

Destination
Document: Collecting Butterflies.in...
Text Anchor: Imago state

When you link to a text anchor, you get the options to choose a document destination and a text anchor in that document.

Setting a paragraph cross-reference

Paragraph cross-references are incredibly versatile. As long as you have previously applied paragraph styles to text, you can easily create cross-references to those paragraphs. (They are of no use, however, if you don't use paragraph styles.) After you choose Paragraph for the Link To option, you can then choose the document for the cross-reference. Underneath, on the left, you see all the paragraph styles in the document. Choose the style that governs the text that you want to link to. For instance, if you want to refer to a chapter title, you would choose the paragraph style applied to all chapter titles.

Once you choose a paragraph style, all the text with that paragraph style appears on the right. Scroll through the list to find the paragraph that you want to link to. (If your paragraphs are long, you will see only a short section of the text.) Click the text. This sets the link to that paragraph.

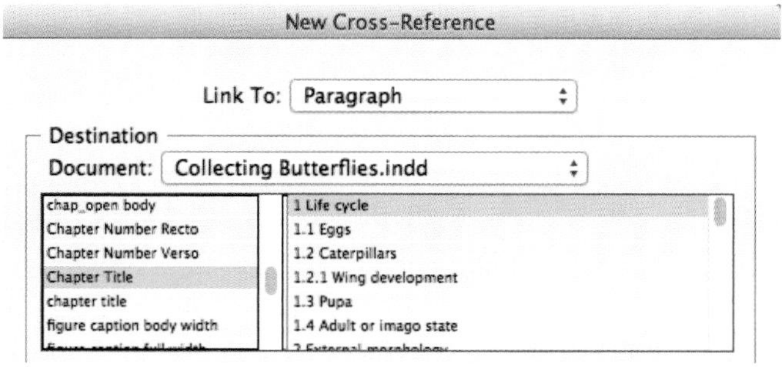

**New Cross-Reference**

Link To: Paragraph

Destination
Document: Collecting Butterflies.indd

| | |
|---|---|
| chap_open body | 1 Life cycle |
| Chapter Number Recto | 1.1 Eggs |
| Chapter Number Verso | 1.2 Caterpillars |
| Chapter Title | 1.2.1 Wing development |
| chapter title | 1.3 Pupa |
| figure caption body width | 1.4 Adult or imago state |
| figure caption full width | 2 External morphology |

When you link to a paragraph, you get the options to choose a document destination and the paragraph styles for the text in the document. You can then choose the specific paragraph you want to link to.

Formatting the text inside the cross-reference

Once you have chosen the Link To and Destination options for the cross-reference, you need to format the text that will be used as the cross-reference. Use the Cross-Reference Format menu to control what text is placed inside the cross-reference.

InDesign ships with seven pre-made cross-reference formats. These formats provide most of the typical text for cross-references. For example, the Page Number format will insert the cross-reference text page <#> into the text. The code <#> is replaced by the actual page number in the document. Here are the pre-made cross-references and the text they insert. The quotation marks are part of the text that is inserted.

TIP There is a setting in the Preflight panel that will alert you if you have missing or unresolved cross references.

| Format Name | Text Inserted |
| --- | --- |
| Full Paragraph & Page Number | "<all the text in the paragraph (including bullets or numbered lists)>" on page <#> |
| Full Paragraph | "<all the text in the paragraph (including bullets or numbered lists)>" |
| Paragraph Text & Page Number | "<all the text in the paragraph (excluding bullets or numbered lists)>" on page <#> |
| Paragraph Text | "<all the text in the paragraph (excluding bullets or numbered lists)>" |
| Paragraph Number & Page Number | <number from a numbered list> on page <#> |
| Paragraph Number | <number from a numbered list> |
| Text Anchor Name & Page Number | "<name of the text anchor>" on page <#> |
| Text Anchor Name | "<name of the text anchor>" |
| Page Number | page <#> |

TIP Use the cross-references that don't insert a number for ePub documents.

Just as you can style hyperlinks, you can also format the appearances of cross-references. These are the same as the options covered in "Setting the style and appearance of hyperlinks" on page 26.

# Creating a Table of Contents (TOC)

Creating a table of contents (TOC) in an InDesign document is like creating a massive set of cross-references. The TOC not only keeps track of the location of a specific paragraph in a document (along with the page number on which it appears), but it also automatically creates electronic links from the text in the TOC to the text in the document. Creating a

TOC also creates bookmarks for PDF documents, which is covered in the section "Working with Bookmarks" on page 39.

Setting the table of contents paragraphs

A TOC simply is simply a list of all the paragraphs in the document that have a certain paragraph style applied. You must, however, create and apply paragraph styles to the text in your document in order to generate a TOC.

Once you have the paragraph styles applied to the text in your document, choose Layout > Table of Contents. This opens the Table of Contents dialog box.

TIP The entire TOC generated by the dialog box is one complete area of the text linked to the paragraphs in the document. The TOC can be edited once it is created, but those edits will be discarded if you update the TOC. That's why it is important to use all the electronic features in the Table of Contents dialog box to create and format the text.

Setting the Title listing

At the top of the Table of Contents dialog box, you'll see the Title field. This is simply the text that will be inserted to label the table of contents. The default is "Contents," but you can substitute any text you want. For instance, we used the title "In This Chapter" for the TOC we put at the front of each chapter of this book.

The Style menu to the right of the Title field allows you to set the paragraph style for the title text. Once again, this paragraph style needs to be defined ahead of time.

TIP An often-requested feature is the ability to select character styles for TOC listings. Unfortunately, this is not currently available in InDesign.

The Table of Contents dialog box is where you choose the paragraph styles and settings for the TOC. In this case, the chapter titles and a heads are used to create the TOC.

**Choosing the listings for the TOC**

The **Styles in Table of Contents** area is the main area where you choose which text will be numbered. The right side of this area has a list of styles called **Other Styles**. This is a list of all paragraph styles in your document.

Click the name of a style that you want listed in the TOC, and then click the **Add** button. This moves the style name from Other Styles to the **Include Paragraph Styles** area. For instance, if you want the chapter titles to appear in the TOC, you would choose the paragraph style applied to the chapter titles. (This is why using descriptive names for your paragraph styles is important.) Continue with the rest of the styles that you want to add to the TOC.

**Styling the TOC listings**

The paragraph styles now need to be styled. Click the name of one of the paragraph styles in the **Include Paragraph Styles** area. Under the section Style: [name of style], you'll see the **Entry Style** menu. Once again, this is a list of all the styles in your document. Unlike the styles that you selected to be the listings in the TOC, this menu is used to format those listings. If you want the TOC list to use the same formatting that appears in the document, leave the setting as [Same Style]. If not, select a paragraph style from the list. We like to style the TOC with its own paragraph styles since most of our chapter titles are far too big to use in a TOC. Continue by selecting the next paragraph style and setting the Entry Style for that listing.

**Opening the rest of the options**

Just when you think you're finished choosing and formatting the styles for the TOC, there are still other formatting options. Click the **More Options** button. This opens up the rest of the Table of Contents dialog box.

The additional options for styling the listings in a TOC.

**Controlling the page numbers**

With the additional options available, you can control the position and style of the page number for the entry listing. Use the Page Number menu to choose one of the following:

- **After Entry** positions the number after the end of the text for the listing.
- **Before Entry** positions the number before the start of the text for the listing.
- **No Page Number** deletes the page number from the listing. This option can be used for ePubs, which don't have page numbers. It

can also be used to create lists of items formatted with a specific paragraph style.

Use the Style menu to the right of the Page Number menu to apply a character style to the numbers in the list. Or you can leave this setting as [None], which leaves the numbers styled with the paragraph style for the entry.

TIP We like to create two different styles for the numbers: plain black text for documents that will be printed, and blue text for interactive links in PDF documents.

The Style menu that applies character styles to the page numbers in a TOC.

The Between Entry and Number field allows you to enter the characters that separate the entry and the page number. The default setting is the code for a tab character (^t), but you can enter any character you want. Click the triangle to the right of the field to open the menu of characters. These include the various space characters, em and en dashes, bullets, tabs, forced line breaks, and the end nested style character.

But you aren't limited to inserting just the items in the menu. You can type your own characters in the field. For instance, if you want the word "Page" to appear before the page number, just type the word and a space after the code for the tab character.

Use the Style menu to the right of the Between Entry and Number field to style those characters with a character style sheet. This can be very helpful if you have a tab leader character, such as a period, filling in the space between the entry and the page number. In that case, you might want to apply a character style that reduces the size and increases the tracking between the periods.

Setting the TOC levels  It's strange that Adobe included a setting for the levels of the items in a TOC, because it only indented extries if they were sorted alphabetically. Other than that it would just indent the items in the Include Paragraph Styles list. There, the levels made it easy to see each type of listing in the TOC, but the setting was for cosmetic purposes only. If you wanted the items to be indented in the actual TOC, you had to set a paragraph style that indented those items.

The Level setting in the Table of Contents dialog box indents the listings for the paragraphs to be included in the TOC. Here, the listing for the chapter title has a level 1 setting, while the listing for the a head has a level 2 setting.

But all that is different with the output to ePubs. When you set the levels for each listing in a TOC, you also control the indents and nesting for the items in the electronic TOC in an exported ePub. When you set the levels in the TOC, those levels can then be used in the electronic TOC that is created for the ePub. This is handled when you create a table of Contents style. (*See page 38 to learn how to create a Table of Contents style.*)

Entries in an ePub nested in the electronic TOC generated from the TOC in InDesign.

Sorting the TOC entries

A TOC doesn't have to be in the order that the items appear in the document. You could, for example, have a TOC list of all the names of the photographers in your book. In that case you might want to alphabetize the list to make it easier to find a specific person. Just select **Sort Entries in Alphabetical Order**.

Setting the TOC options

Additional controls for creating a TOC are found under the Options area.

The Options area for the Table of Contents dialog box.

### Create PDF Bookmarks

Bookmarks are navigational controls that appear on the side of a PDF document in Reader or Acrobat. Select the option Create PDF Bookmarks to automatically add these to the InDesign Bookmarks panel. The bookmarks can then be exported as part of the PDF. (*See the next section, "Working with Bookmarks," for more information.*)

### Replace Existing Table of Contents

Choose this option if you already have created a TOC in the document and now want to replace it with a new one with new formatting and styles. This is different from the Update Table of Contents command in the Layout menu. That command retains all the elements in the TOC but updates the text and page numbers.

### Include Book Documents

This command is available only if a Book file is open. Then the TOC that you create will list all the entries in all the documents in the book.

### Setting a TOC to run as a single paragraph

Select the Run-in option to set the entries as a single paragraph. The entries are separated by a semicolon (;) and a space.

### Including non-printing text

The entries for a TOC don't have to be visible in the finished document. Select the option Include Text on Hidden Layers to create a list of items such as the copyright information for photographs or illustrations.

### Working with numbered paragraphs

If you have TOC entries that come from numbered paragraphs, you can control how those numbers are handled.

- **Include Full Paragraph** includes the text and its number.
- **Include Numbers Only** includes just the numbers for the paragraph.
- **Exclude Numbers** includes the text but not the numbers.

*Flowing the table of contents text*

Once you have set the paragraph styles for the TOC, click the OK button to close the dialog box. You should now have a cursor loaded with the TOC text.

Click to place the TOC text on a page. There are no indicators on the layout that the text is linked to other pages, but as with hyperlinks, you can see the link markers in the Story Editor. Of course, if you export as a PDF or ePub, the hyperlinks do work.

*Creating a Table of Contents style*

There is a special feature of the TOC that makes it easy to apply all the settings in the Table of Contents dialog box to other documents. But more importantly for digital publications, it is used for creating navigation for an ePub. In an ePub, you can create an list for all the chapters or headers in your document. The reader then clicks the entry in the list to jump to a new section of the book. This navigational list comes from creating and saving a TOC style for the document.

It's very simple to create a TOC style. Just set up the Table of Contents dialog box with the paragraphs that you want in the navigation list. Click the Save Style button and name the TOC style. You don't have to actually create a TOC. You only need the style settings captured under a style name. Then, when you create the ePub for the document, you can choose the TOC style to create the navigational list. (*See Chapter 6, "ePubs and HTML," to learn how to create ePub documents.*)

# Working with Bookmarks

Bookmarks are used only in PDF documents. They provide a different way to navigate within a document. Instead of being elements on the page, bookmarks are displayed in the Acrobat or Reader Bookmarks pane. The reader clicks each bookmark to move to that position in the document. One of the advantages to using bookmarks is that the Bookmarks pane can always be visible next to the area being read.

Bookmarks in Adobe Reader and Adobe Acrobat let the user easily navigate to pages in the document.

*Creating individual bookmarks*

To create individual bookmarks, choose Window > Interactive > Bookmarks to open the Bookmarks panel.

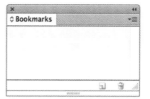

The Bookmarks panel as it first appears.

You can create various types of bookmarks, depending on what you select first:

- Place the insertion point within the text and click the New Bookmark icon. This creates a generically named text bookmark.
- Select the text and click the New Bookmark icon. This creates a text bookmark named with the selected text.
- Select a frame or graphic and click the New Bookmark icon. This creates a page bookmark.
- Click a page in the Pages panel and click the New Bookmark icon. This creates a page bookmark.

**Nesting bookmarks**

You may have a lot of bookmarks in a document. Instead of scrolling through a long list of those bookmarks, you can *nest* them, or move bookmarks so they are contained within others. The top bookmark is called the *parent*; the nested bookmark is called the *child*. This not only shortens the list of bookmarks, it shows the structure of how some items are sub-heads of the others in the list.

Drag the bookmark you want to nest onto the name of the parent bookmark. When the name is highlighted, release the mouse button. The child bookmark is indented under the parent. A triangle controller appears that lets you open or close the parent bookmark.

The Bookmarks panel with nested bookmarks. These bookmarks were created automatically by creating a table of contents in the document.

**Getting bookmarks from a table of contents**

You don't have to manually create bookmarks. You can automatically generate bookmarks by creating a table of contents for the document. When you create the table of contents, select the option **Create PDF Bookmarks** in the Table of Contents dialog box. The bookmarks are automatically added to the Bookmarks panel.

As soon as you create the loaded cursor for the table of contents, the bookmarks appear in the panel. Click to place the table of contents text on a page.

You must keep the table of contents in the document. If you delete it, the bookmarks are deleted from the panel.

TIP If you don't want the table of contents in your document, you can put its text on a non-printing, hidden layer. This keeps the bookmarks in the panel without showing the table of contents.

# Working with Object States

Another type of interactive element is the multi-state object. A multi-state object allows you to show a series of frames in a slideshow-style display. Multi-state objects are used only in SWF or DPS app files. You create multi-state objects using the Object States panel.

Creating a multi-state object

Choose Window > Interactive > Object States to open the Object States panel. Select the objects for the multi-state object. You can have a variety of objects in each state.

For instance, you can have an image in the first state, text that describes the image in the next, and a movie that features that image in the next. You can also combine objects for each state as long as you group them before converting them into a state.

Left: A stack of objects ready to be converted into a multi-state object. Right: The same objects converted into a multi-state object.

TIP Make all the objects the same size to create the effect of one object changing into another.

TIP Use the Align Centers command to have the states appear in the same position.

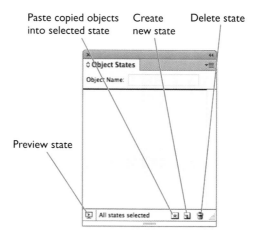

The Object States panel without any states.

Once all of your objects or grouped objects are aligned on top of each other, click the **Convert Selection To Multi-State Object** button. This puts each object into its own state, which appears in the Object States panel.

TIP Hold the Opt/Alt key to put all the objects into a single state.

The Object States panel with a multi-state object selected.

Editing a multi-state object

Once you have created a multi-state object, you can make changes to each state, make changes to the object as a whole, edit the content of a state, or add states.

To edit the multi-state object as a whole, use the Selection tool to select the multi-state object on the page. The icon in the Object States panel indicates that the entire multi-state object has been selected. Then make whatever edits you want to the object. All the states will be modified. For instance, if you change the size of the object, the size of all the states will change.

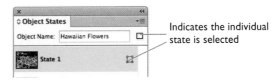

Indicates the multi-state
object as a whole is selected

The Object States panel with three states visible. The multi-state object is selected.

To edit a single state, select the state in the Object States panel. The indicator icon in the panel indicates that just that specific state has been selected. Make whatever changes you want to the object. Only that specific state will be modified.

Indicates the individual
state is selected

The Object States panel with an individual state selected.

To edit the content of a state, select the state in the Object States panel. Then use the Direct Selection tool to select the content of the state. The indicator icon in the panel changes to show that the content of the state is selected. Make the changes you want.

Indicates the content of
the state is selected

The Object States panel with the content of a state selected.

To add an object to an existing state, select both the new object and the multi-state object and then click the **Add Objects to Visible State** button.

To add an object as a new state in an existing multi-state object, select both the object and the multi-state object. Then click the **Convert Selection to Multi-State Object** button.

Add objects to visible state

Convert selection to multi-state object

The Object States panel with a multi-state object and an ordinary object selected.

- To duplicate a state, select a state and then choose **New State** from the Object States panel menu.
- To paste objects into an existing state, cut or copy one or more objects, select the multi-state object, select the state in the Object States panel, and choose **Paste Into State** from the Object States panel menu.
- To convert a single state back to an object on the page, select the state in the Object States panel and choose **Release State to Object** from the panel menu.
- To convert all states in the multi-state object to objects, choose **Release All States to Objects** from the panel menu.
- To delete a state and remove its contents, select the state and click the **Delete State** button or choose **Delete State** from the panel menu.

Using buttons to display object states

Once you have created a multi-state object, you can use the actions in buttons to cycle forward and back through the object states or jump to specific object states. (*See the section "Our Favorite Button Effects" for an exercise on how to create these buttons.*)

Hiding multi-state objects until triggered

You use buttons to cycle through the states of a multi-state object. However, there may be times when you don't want the object to be seen until the button to show the states is activated. To hide the multi-state object until it's triggered by a button, choose Hidden Until Triggered from the panel menu.

TIP The first state visible is the state that is selected when the file is saved.

Previewing and testing multi-state objects

To see how a multi-state object works, you use the SWF Preview panel. For more information on using the Preview panel, see Chapter 3, "Animations."

TIP You use interactive buttons to trigger each of the object states. See "Creating Buttons" on page 51.

The SWF Preview panel is used to preview the buttons that trigger the display of multi-state objects.

# Audio and Video Formats

For many of us coming from the print world, it's surprising how enjoyable it is working with sounds and movies in documents. It's thrilling to add clicks to buttons or see our own instructional movies in interactive files.

But not all multimedia formats work in all types of digital publications. Here are some of the most common multimedia file formats and where they can be used.

| File Format | PDF | ePub | SWF | DPS Apps |
| --- | --- | --- | --- | --- |
| FLV | Yes | No | Yes | No |
| F4V | Yes | No | Yes | No |
| MP4 | Yes | Yes | Yes | Yes |
| MP3 | Yes | Yes | Yes | Yes |
| SWF | Yes | No | Yes | No |
| MOV | Yes | Yes | No | Yes |
| AVI | Yes | Yes | No | Yes |
| MPEG | Yes | Yes | No | Yes |

As you can see, the most versatile formats are MP4 (for video) and MP3 (for audio). However, you may have files in other formats that you need to convert. In that case, you can use the Adobe Media Encoder. If you have Adobe Premiere Pro, Adobe Flash Professional, or Adobe Creative Suite Production Premium, the Adobe Media Encoder is automatically installed.

*Converting files using the Adobe Media Encoder*

Open the Media Encoder. Don't let the size of the window overwhelm you. All you need to focus on is the **Queue pane** in the upper-left corner.

Click the plus sign to add files for conversion. Use the Format control to choose the new format for the file. Choose H.264 (Legacy) to create MP4 video files; choose MP3 to create audio files.

When you have added all the files you want to convert, click the **Start Queue button** (green triangle). The new files appear in the location specified in the Output File area.

The Queue pane of the Adobe Media Encoder is where you can convert video and audio files to the correct format for digital publications.

# Working with Audio Files

Despite the mind-bending concept (to a print person) of adding sound to a page layout, it's actually very simple to work with audio files, or sounds. Our favorite use for sounds is as effects that play when a button is clicked. We might also add short bits of music that play when a document is first opened. If you know how to place an image into InDesign, you already know how to place a sound in a document.

TIP As with other interactive elements, not all export formats support playing sounds in documents.

Adding sound files to documents

Choose File > Place, and then choose the sound file you want to import. The cursor changes into the Sound Clip cursor. Click or drag the Sound Clip cursor to add the sound clip to the document.

Once you have the sound clip on the page, use the Media panel to set the options for how the sound plays.

Using the Media panel to set sound options

Choose Window > Interactive > Media. The Media panel appears. Use the panel to apply the sound options.

The Media panel with the sound controls visible.

- **Play on Page Load** sets the sound to automatically play when the page is visible.
- **Stop on Page Turn** sets the sound to automatically stop when the page is no longer visible.
- **Loop** repeats the sound until manually stopped.

**Previewing sounds with the Media panel**

The Media panel also lets you play the sound from start to finish or select specific portions of the sound.

TIP In the exported document, a sound file can be prompted to play by clicking the element, or you can set a button to play the sound. See "Creating Buttons" on page 51 for more information on using buttons to play media.

Select the sound on the page. The Media panel shows the controls and the poster image for the sound.

Click the **Play** button to hear the sound. The playhead moves along the sound play line to indicate the current playback position within the clip. As the sound plays, the Play button is replaced by a Stop button. Click the **Stop** button to stop the playback.

TIP The two time indicators show how far along the playback is and the total length of time of the sound clip.

TIP You can also use the SWF Preview panel to hear sounds.

**Setting the poster for sounds**

When a sound is included on a page, it acts like a button that can play the sound when clicked. So you might want to include a *poster,* or visual indicator, that lets people know there is a sound in that location.

Use the Poster menu to choose an image that will be used to show where the sound is in the document:

- **None** leaves the sound clip frame empty.
- **Standard** uses the standard sound poster image.
- **From File/Choose Image** lets you import a custom image to use as the sound poster. Click the Choose button to choose the custom image.

TIP Not all graphic file formats can be used as a sound poster. We have found that the best choices are pixel-based files, such as JPEGs or PSDs.

The standard sound poster (left) and an image used as a sound poster (right).

# Movies and Videos

One of the more exciting multimedia features is the ability to add movies or videos to digital publications.

TIP Once again, as with other interactive elements, not all export formats support playing videos in documents.

Adding videos to documents

Choose File > Place, and then choose the video file you want to import. The cursor changes into the Video Clip cursor. Click or drag to place the video on the document. This adds a video object to the document.

Once you have the video on the page, you can use the Media panel to modify and set the playback options.

Using the Media panel with videos

Choose Window > Interactive > Media. The Media panel appears. With the video selected, set each of the options.

- Select **Play on Page Load** to play the video automatically when the page is visible.
- Select **Loop (SWF export only)** to repeat the video until manually stopped. This option doesn't apply if the file is exported as a PDF.

TIP In the exported document, a video file can be prompted to play by clicking the element, or you can set a button to play the sound. See "Creating Buttons" on page 51 for more information on using buttons to play media.

The Media panel with an MP4 file selected.

**Setting the poster for movies**

Like sound files, videos act as buttons that play the video when clicked. So you may want to set a poster that appears on the page to let the viewer know that there is a video at that position. Since they are movies, they have more poster options than sound files.

Use the Poster menu to choose an image that will be used to show where the movie is in the document:

- **None** leaves the frame empty.
- **Standard** uses the standard video file icon.
- **From Current Frame** uses the frame currently displayed in the Media panel.
- **Choose Image** lets you import a custom image to use as the movie poster.

**Setting a controller for the video**

Use the Controller menu to apply one of the controllers that can be used to control the playback of the movie, play it in full screen, adjust the sound, and show captions. The name of each controller explains which features it has. For instance, **SkinOverAll** contains all the features for controlling videos. The controller **SkinOverPlay** contains only the Play button.

Select **Show Controller on Rollover** to have the controller appear and disappear when the mouse moves inside and outside the area of the video. When Show Controller on Rollover is not selected, the controller is always visible.

The Media panel also lets you preview a movie from start to finish or move to specific portions of the movie. To preview a movie using the Media panel, click the **Play** button to play the movie within the Preview area of the Media panel. As the movie plays, the Play button is replaced by a **Pause** button. Click the Pause button to stop the playback.

TIP The two time indicators show the current playback location and the total length of time of the movie.

Streaming videos to documents

When you place a video onto an InDesign page, the video is embedded in the exported file. But video files take up a lot of space and may not be practical to include in a PDF that will be emailed to someone. That's when you can use the option to place a video from a URL. As handy as this technique is, it works only with videos that are exported as PDF files; it doesn't work for DPS applications.

Create an empty frame on the page. It helps if the frame has the same aspect ratio as the video. With the frame selected, choose **Video from URL** from the Media panel menu. This opens the Place Video from URL dialog box, which allows you to set the URL path for the video. This needs to be a complete path to the video file, such as http://www.domain.com/videos/videofile.mp4. Once you have created the link to the URL, you can choose a poster for the file and set the other video options.

The video must be one of the formats that can be played by the Flash Player. But if you are working with files for the iPad or another device that doesn't read SWF files, then you need to use the MP4 format.

Controlling movies in PDF documents

If a movie file is going to be used in a PDF document, there are some additional controls you can set.

To set the options for a video in a PDF document, click the **Export Interactive PDF** icon on the Media panel or choose PDF Options from the Media panel menu. This opens the PDF Options dialog box.

In the **Description** field, enter the text that will be used as a tool tip for the video clip. This text is also heard by visually impaired users who use screen readers to listen to the text in a document.

Click **Play Video in Floating Window** to display the video in a separate window above the PDF file. If you have the video play in a floating window, you can set a size for the display. Use the Size list to choose a size, such as 1/5 of the video or 2 times the size of the video. If you have chosen a QuickTime MOV file, you can also set the position of the video to the corners or center of the screen.

TIP The MOV file format can be used only in interactive PDF files, not SWF documents.

# Creating Buttons

Like hyperlinks, buttons can send the user to destinations. But buttons are more powerful than simple hyperlinks. Buttons contain the code that can link you to destinations, flip pages in a document, open web pages, play movies, show and hide other buttons, and do other tricks.

You use the Buttons and Forms panel to create and apply actions to buttons. Choose Window > Interactive > Buttons and Forms to open the panel. There are two types of interactive elements that can be created in the Buttons and Forms panel: *Buttons* are objects that apply actions; *forms* are objects that allow the user to enter text or click to set the status of the field. We'll look at buttons first and look at forms in the next section.

*Creating and naming a button*

Select an object. Any object, except media files, can be used as a button. Choose Object > Interactive > Convert to Button, or click the **Convert Object to Button** icon in the Buttons and Forms panel. The object is converted into a button and displays the button icon.

Use the **Name** field in the Buttons and Forms panel to change the default name to something more descriptive. It's helpful to name buttons with their functions. For example, buttons that move the viewer to the previous page or next page would be labeled Previous Page and Next Page.

TIP You can remove the button properties from an object by selecting the button and either choosing Object > Interactive > Convert to Object or clicking the Convert Button to Object icon in the Buttons and Forms panel.

If you create a button for a PDF document, you should open the PDF Options area and fill in the **Description** field. Type a description or tool tip that explains to the viewer the function of the button. For example, if the button moves the reader to the next page, the description might say "Click to move to the next page."

The Description field is also the text that is read by electronic screen reader devices for visually impaired users. You may be required by law to add these descriptions to your documents. (*See Chapter 7, "Exporting PDF and SWF" for more information on setting descriptions in PDF documents.*)

## Section 508 Accesibility

The tool tip description for PDF documents is one of the accessibility settings for electronic documents that are required by many government agencies under Section 508 of an amendment signed in 1998 to the Workforce Rehabilitation Act of 1973. (Many countries outside the US require similar accessibility options for electronic documents.)

If you do work for a department of the US government — or any part of your company works with the US government — you need to make your electronic documents accessible. In addition, companies may require that documentation for human resources and other departments be accessible under the Americans with Disabilites Act.

And aside from the laws, it's only polite to create description tool tips in your PDF documents.

The Buttons and Forms panel with a button selected.

**Adding events to buttons**

A button without an action is like a light switch that's not connected to a lamp. You can click the switch all you want, but nothing's going to happen. There are two parts to setting actions. First you use the **Event** menu to choose what type of mouse or keyboard action will prompt the button to perform the action.

- **On Release or Tap** applies an action under two circumstances: when the mouse button is released after a click and when a tablet screen is tapped.
- **On Click** applies an action as the mouse button is pressed down.
- **On Roll Over** applies an action when the mouse cursor is moved over the button's bounding box.
- **On Roll Off** applies an action when the mouse cursor is moved away from the button's bounding box.
- **On Focus (PDF)** applies an action when the Tab key is used to jump onto the button. Jumping onto the button is called putting the focus on the button. On Focus works only for buttons in PDF documents, where you can press the Tab key to navigate.
- **On Blur (PDF)** applies an action when the Tab key is used to jump off the button. In this case, the term blur is used as the opposite of focus, although the button's visibility doesn't actually change. On Blur works only for buttons in PDF documents, where you can press the Tab key to navigate.

TIP You can set multiple events for a button. For example, a button can play a sound when the mouse rolls over it but open a web page when it is clicked.

**Choosing actions for buttons**

Once you have chosen the mouse event, you then choose the *action* that follows the event. Not all actions can be used with all types of exported files.

Even if the action is listed for all media, some actions may work in some ePub readers but not others. For example, videos can play in iBooks but not on Android readers.

| Action | Description | Used for |
|---|---|---|
| Go To Destination | Goes to a previously defined text anchor. | All exported media except DPS apps |
| Go To First Page, Last Page, Next Page, Previous Page | Goes to the first page, last page, next page, or previous page. | All exported media. Next Page and Previous Page are not supported in DPS apps. |
| Go To URL | Goes to a web page or the action specified in the URL. | All exported media |
| Show/Hide Buttons and Forms | Reveals or hides a previously defined button or form . | All exported media except DPS apps |

| Action | Description | Used for |
|--------|-------------|----------|
| Sound | Adds the controls to play, pause, stop, or resume playing a sound placed in the document. | All exported media |
| Video | Adds the controls to play, pause, stop, or resume playing a video placed in the document. | All exported media |
| Animation | Adds the controls to play, pause, stop, or resume playing an animation created from InDesign objects on the page. *For more information on creating animations, see Chapter 3.* | SWF. Available for DPS apps only via HTML5 conversion. |
| Go To Page | Goes to a specific page. | DPS apps and SWF only |
| Go To State | Goes to a specific state in a multi-state object. | DPS apps and SWF only |
| Go To Next State, Previous State | Goes to the next state or previous state in a multi-state object. | DPS apps and SWF only |
| Clear Form | Resets form fields in the PDF page to their default values. | PDF only |
| Go To Next View, Previous View | Goes to the previous view or next view in the PDF. | PDF only |
| Open File | Opens an external file. You must specify an absolute pathname, such as C:\docs\sample.pdf. | PDF only |
| Print Form | Opens the Print dialog box to print the contents of a PDF page with form data. | PDF only |
| Submit Form | Opens a dialog box that lets the reader choose how to email a PDF page with form data. The URL field for this action needs to be an email link, such as mailto:person@domain.com. | PDF only |
| View Zoom | Displays the page according to one of the PDF zoom options. | PDF only |

**Applying actions to events**

With the event selected, click the **Add Action** icon in the Actions area of the Buttons panel. This displays the Actions menu.

Choose the action that you want to apply. The action appears in the Actions area of the Buttons panel. Depending on the action, additional controls may appear in the Buttons panel. Set those controls as necessary. Repeat these steps to apply more actions to the form.

Add action                 Delete action

Name: Button 2

Event: On Release or Tap

Actions:

☑ Go To Next State (Hawaiin Plants 2)

☑ Go To First Page

Click the Add Action or Delete Action icon to apply or delete the actions applied to events.

To delete the action for a button event, select the action in the Actions area and click the **Delete Action** icon.

TIP Instead of deleting an action, you can disable it by deselecting the check box next to its name. This keeps the action available, but the action does not export with the button.

If you have multiple actions for an event, the actions are applied in the order that they appear in the list. Drag the action up or down in the Actions list to change the order in which the actions are applied. This order can be important when playing sounds and movies. For instance, you might want the action for a click sound to play before the action to play a movie.

Button appearances

One of the benefits to working with buttons is the ability to change their appearance so that the button itself responds to the actions of the user. This means that the button can change its color when the mouse presses down, or the button can "wake up" with a glow when the cursor passes over the button boundary. However, the best appearance changes are subtle.

When you create a button, it has only one appearance, called the **Normal** state. There are two additional states: **Rollover** and **Click**. The Normal state is the appearance of the button when the mouse is not near it. The Rollover state is the appearance of the button when the mouse cursor enters the button area. The Click state is the appearance of the button when the mouse presses down on the button. Only the Normal and Click states are used in DPS apps.

Creating button appearances

The following exercise shows how to create the appearance for a button that starts as a native InDesign object.

**55**

1. Use the Buttons and Forms panel to convert the object into a button. This automatically creates the Normal state. The selections for Rollover and Click are empty.

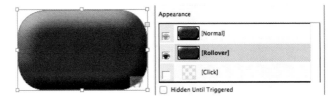

The Normal state of a button in the Appearance area of the Buttons and Forms panel.

2. To create the Rollover state, click its listing in the panel. This adds the Rollover state appearance that contains the same artwork as the Normal state.

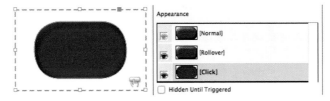

The Normal state duplicated into the Rollover state of a button.

3. To modify the appearance of the Rollover state, keep it selected in the panel and change the size, shape, or effects applied to the object.

4. Click the listing for the Click state in the panel. This adds the Click state to the panel. It too contains the same artwork as the Normal state.

5. To modify the appearance of the Click state, keep it selected in the panel and change its size, shape, or effects.

The Click state modified from the Normal state.

One of the effects we like to create for the Rollover state is the look that the button is moving up, toward the viewer. We create a Normal state and then add the Rollover appearance. We then increase the size of the Rollover state, lighten the color, and add a slight drop shadow. We also modify the Click state so that it looks like it is moving down, away from the viewer. For that look we decrease the size of the button, darken the color, and remove the drop shadow.

## Appearances versus actions

You may be confused about the difference between appearance and action for the Rollover and Click states. Both respond to the user moving into the area of the button or clicking the button. So what's the difference?

Button appearances are limited to displaying the look of the new state. The user moves into the area of the button, and the appearance of the Rollover state is displayed. Or the user clicks the button, and the appearance of the Click state is shown. But that's it. Applying a button appearance doesn't do anything except change the look of that button.

Button actions do things—change the page, play a movie, show a field. Actions can be applied to any of the button events. It just so happens that the names of those events—On Rollover and On Click—are the same as the events that show the button appearances.

This means you can have a Rollover appearance that displays a glow around the button. You can also have an action applied to the Rollover event that plays a sound. Two distinct things happen—one for the appearance and the other for the action.

**Applying text to button states**

You can also use text as a button. For instance, you can have buttons that are labeled "Stop," "Play," "Print," or whatever action has been assigned to the button. Select the text frame and convert it to a button. This creates the Normal state. Create any additional appearances as necessary.

**Using imported images for button states**

We like to use images created in Adobe Photoshop or Adobe Illustrator for buttons.

Start by selecting the images you want to use. Most of the time we use images that are all the same size. This creates the effect of one state of the button magically changing to another state when the button is rolled over, clicked, or tapped. You can resize the artwork after you create the button, but it is easier to do so before you create each state.

1. Select the image for the Normal appearance and convert the object to a button. This converts that image to the Normal state in the Buttons and Forms panel.

2. Add the Rollover or Click state to the button. This duplicates the image from the Normal state into the Rollover or Click state.

3. Move the Selection tool cursor over the button so you see the Content Grabber (circle). Click to select the image, and delete it. An empty graphics frame appears.

4. Select the image you want to use for the Rollover or Click appearance. Copy or Cut the image to the clipboard.

5. Select the Rollover or Click appearance in the Buttons and Forms panel.

6. Double-click the button frame so that it has a solid frame rather than the dotted button-indication frame.

7. From the Edit menu, choose the **Paste Into** command. The new image becomes the Rollover or Click appearance for the button.

TIP You can also use the Place command to import an image directly into the appearance state.

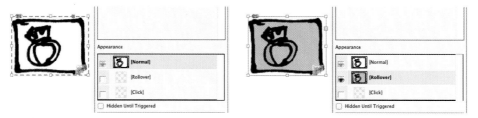

To use a different image in the Rollover or Click appearance, use the Paste Into command.

TIP Instead of using the Paste Into command to change the image in a button, you can create separate layers in a Photoshop or Illustrator file by putting each image on its own layer. Once you use the image in a new state, select the object and then choose Object > Object Layers to turn the layers on or off for the image you wish to use.

Deleting or hiding button states

Select the Rollover or Click state and click the **Delete State** icon. You can't delete the Normal state.

Instead of deleting states, which tosses out their content, it may be better to change whether or not the state is exported. To change the visibility of a state, click the eyeball icon next to the name of the state. If the eyeball is visible, it means the state is enabled and will export. If the eyeball is not visible, it means the state is disabled and will not export. The exception to this rule is the Normal state, which is always visible and can't be deleted.

# Our Favorite Button Effects

With the various events and actions, there are literally thousands of ways to work with buttons. Rather than try to cover them all, here are two step-by-step exercises for creating our favorite button effects.

Show/hide rollover effect

This exercise creates an effect wherein moving the mouse over a small image reveals a larger version of that image. Because it relies on a button rollover, it is available only for interactive PDF and SWF output.

1. Start by creating two buttons. Place both the small and large images on the page. Select each image and convert it to a button. We like to name the small image "Image Trigger" and the large image "Image Target."

2. With the Image Trigger button selected, set the event to On Roll Over. This sets the button to respond when the mouse enters the area of the button.

3. You now want to add an action to the Image Trigger button. With the Image Trigger button still selected, click the Add New Action icon. Then choose Show/Hide Buttons and Forms from the Actions menu. When you choose this action, the panel expands to show the added controls for the Show/Hide Buttons and Forms action.

4. Set the visibility of the Image Trigger button's On Roll Over event. The visibility controls for the Show/Hide action allow you to set whether buttons are hidden or shown when the event happens. All the buttons and forms in the document are listed in the Visibility area. Click the Show icon at the bottom of the Visibility area. This means that when the mouse rolls over the Image Trigger button, the Image Target button will be displayed. Understand that you are working on the Image Trigger button but setting the visibility of the Image Target button.

The On Roll Over visibility settings for a Show/Hide button

5. Now that you have set the On Roll Over event and action, you need to set the On Roll Off behaviors. This is necessary so that the Image Target disappears when the mouse leaves the area of the Image Trigger. With the Image Trigger button still selected, set the event to On Roll Off.

6. Choose Show/Hide Buttons and Forms from the Actions menu.

7. Click the Hide icon at the bottom of the visibility area. This means that when the mouse moves away from the button area, the Image Target button will be hidden.

The On Roll Off visibility settings for a Show/Hide button.

8. There's one more setting that is necessary. At the moment, the Image Target will be seen when the page opens. You want it to be hidden until the mouse rolls over the Image Trigger. Select the Image Target button, and select the option **Hidden Until Triggered**. You only need to select this one option for the button.

Using the rollover on one button to show or hide a separate button. When the mouse is off the button, the large image is hidden. When the mouse is inside the area of the button, the large image is displayed.

**Creating buttons to show object states**

This exercise creates a button that cycles through all the states in a multi-state object, and creates other buttons that display a specific state in the multi-state object. The images displayed by the buttons are in different positions on the page. Because these buttons use actions for object states, they do not play in PDF files. They work beautifully, however, in DPS apps.

1. Start by placing the images where you want them on the page. In this example, we have a full map of the United States, as well as maps for the North, South, Midwest, and West of the country. We arrange the full map in the center of the page, with the sections offset slightly.

TIP It's easy to display these separate areas by putting each one on its own layer in Illustrator or Photoshop and then turning those layers on and off using Object > Object Layer Options in InDesign.

Stacking the images for a multi-state object. Here, the areas of a map of the United States are stacked into position.

2. With all the images selected, click the New Multi-state Object button in the Object States panel. This combines each image into its own object state. The states are positioned as they were before being converted into the multi-state object.

TIP The order of the object states comes from the stacking order of the original image. The top image becomes the first state, and so on down the list. Also, the top object state is, by default, the object displayed in the interactive file.

3. For the sake of your sanity, click to change the object name of the multi-state object. We call ours "Map of the US." Also, change each object state's name from its default to the name of its area. This is especially important if you are working in a file with many multi-state objects with many object states.

TIP You can change the name of the object state with a "slow" double-click. Click once on the object state's name, pause a moment, and then click again. The name field will be available for you to type in a new name.

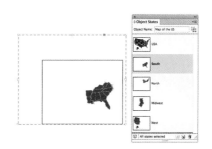

The Object States panel with one of the object states visible. Notice that the object state is positioned in the lower-right corner of the multi-state object.

4. Next create five text frames. One has the label "USA" for the entire map. The others have the labels "North," "South," "Midwest," and "West" for the four sections of the map. Select each frame and

convert it into a button by clicking the Convert to Button icon at the bottom of the Buttons and Forms panel.

5. If the page is going to be used as an interactive SWF file, you can set the appearance for the Rollover effect of the button. Click the Rollover state in the Buttons and Forms panel. This duplicates the text from the Normal state into the Rollover state. Highlight the text in the Rollover state and change it to red. If the page is only going to be used in a DPS application, there is no use for the Rollover effect for the button.

Five buttons created to show the states of a multi-state object. The South button displays the Rollover state. The other buttons show the Normal state.

6. You now need to create the actions for the buttons. Start by selecting the USA button, and set the event to On Release or Tap. This is the only event that is recognized by tablet screens.

7. Click the **Add Action** icon in the Buttons and Forms panel. Choose **Go To Next State** from the menu. Since you have only one multi-state object in the document, the Object menu will automatically list that object. Make sure **Stop at Last State** is deselected. This will allow the button to cycle through all the states and then start again at the first.

The setting for a button that will cycle through all the states in a multi-state object.

8. The other buttons display the specific states of the multi-state object. Select one of the area buttons (North, South, and so on), and set its event to On Release or Tap. Then click the Add Action icon and choose Go To State from the Actions menu. The Object menu displays the multi-state object.

9. Click the State menu to show the five object states. Choose the appropriate state for the button.

The setting for a button that will display a specific state in a multi-state object.

10. Repeat steps 8 and 9 for the rest of the buttons.

11. Use the SWF Preview panel to preview how the buttons display the object states.

TIP If the preview of the images is blurry, choose Edit Preview Settings from the SWF Preview menu. *See Chapter 7, "Exporting PDF and SWF," for details on these settings.*

# Creating PDF Forms

Most likely you've gotten a PDF where you click inside areas of the form and fill them out with the information requested. InDesign lets you add form fields to your documents so you can create these types of interactive PDF files without having to open Acrobat. Just as with buttons, you use the Buttons and Forms panel to create forms.

TIP While buttons can be used on PDF, SWF, and DPS documents, forms can be used only on interactive PDF documents.

A PDF document with interactive form fields.

Creating and
naming forms

Select an object. Any object, except media files, can be used as a form. Choose Object > Interactive > Convert to [form name], or choose one of the types of forms from the Type menu in the Buttons and Forms panel. The following are the types of forms available:

- **A Check Box** creates a Normal On state and a Normal Off state that set on or off options for the form. Set the appearance for each state to create the display of the check box. If there are multiple check boxes, the viewer can select as many as desired.
- **A Combo Box** lets the user choose a value from a menu. This could be a favorite hobby or the way they commute to work. Use the List Items field to enter the items for the menu.
- **A List Box** lets the user choose a value from a list of terms. This could be something like countries the user has visited or classes the user wants to take. Use the List Items field to enter the items for the list.
- **A Signature Field** creates a field where the user can electronically sign a PDF document.
- **Radio buttons** come in groups of buttons. The user can select only one button in the group. If one is selected, the other buttons are deselected. All radio buttons with the same name work together as a group. Style the Normal On or Normal Off states for how the button looks when clicked on or off.
- **A Text field** lets the user enter their own custom text, such as name, address, or phone number.

Use the **Name** field in the Buttons and Forms panel to change the default name to something more descriptive. Leave the Event setting as **On Release or Tap**. Fill in the **Description** field with the text that will be used as a tool tip for the form field. This also lets visually impaired users hear a description of what the form field does.

Setting the options
for forms

There are different options that appear when you choose each type of form. Here are the options and the types of forms they are applied to.

| Option | Function | Used in |
|--------|----------|---------|
| Printable | Allows the field to be printed. | All forms |
| Required | Hides the field's content as a series of asterisks. The contents of the field is exported as real data. Note: At the time of this writing there is a bug in InDesign that allows forms to be submitted even though text fields are set as Required. The fix is to set the fields as Required in Acrobat. | All forms |

| Option | Function | Used in |
|---|---|---|
| Password | Hides the field's content as a series of asterisks. | Text fields |
| Read Only | Prevents the contents of the field from being modified. | All forms |
| Multiline | Allows text to wrap to multiple lines. | Text fields |
| Scrollable | Applies scroll bars if the contents exceed the depth of the field. Scroll bars are automatically applied to combo boxes and list boxes even if this option is unavailable or not selected. | Text fields, combo boxes, and list boxes |
| Selected by Default | Applies the selection when the PDF document is opened. | Check boxes and radio buttons |
| Sort Items | Arranges the list items alphabetically or numerically. | Combo boxes and list boxes |
| Multiple Items | Allows the user to select more than one item in the list by pressing the Shift or Cmd/Ctrl key and clicking the additional items. | List boxes |

**Applying actions to form events**

This feature adds great flexibility to working with forms. You can add an action to what happens when a form field is clicked or rolled over. The action is added to the form using the same steps as you would use to apply an action to a button: Click the Add Action icon in the Actions area of the Buttons panel, and choose an action from the Actions menu. (*For more information on working with actions, see the section on choosing actions for buttons on page 53.*)

There are many ways to use actions with forms—too many to cover here. But one way we like to apply actions to forms is to create radio buttons that display other fields when clicked.

In our example, three radio buttons represent the state where the user lives and three list boxes represent the major areas in that state. The list boxes are stacked on top of each other, and the setting Hidden Until Triggered is chosen. The action Show/Hide Buttons and Forms is applied to the radio buttons so that when the radio button for one state is chosen, the list box for that state is shown and the other list boxes are hidden. Instead of scrolling through a long list of cities, the user is directed to choose from a smaller list.

| NY | NJ | CT | NY | NJ | CT |

Bronx          Newark
Manhattan      Hoboken
Queens         North Bergen
Staten Island  Fort Lee

Actions applied to radio buttons can show or hide other form fields on a page. When the radio button for New York is chosen, the list box that displays the boroughs of New York appears. When the radio button for New Jersey is chosen, the list box for New Jersey cities appears and the other list boxes are hidden.

**Form formatting**

One of the advantages to creating form fields in InDesign is the ability to add fills, strokes, special effects, and imported graphics to the field. These options are not available when creating form fields in Acrobat Pro. Unfortunately, not all of these options are available for all form fields.

You can apply any effect or formatting to form fields, and they will display on the InDesign page. Note that only fills and strokes are maintained in text fields, signature fields, list boxes, and combo boxes when the PDF is exported and opened in Acrobat or Reader; only radio buttons and check boxes maintain all the formatting applied in InDesign.

**Radio buttons and check boxes appearance states**

Unlike ordinary buttons, which only have three appearance states (Normal, Rollover, and Click), radio buttons and check boxes have six states. This is because you may want different information in the field depending on whether or not the form has been selected. The choices are as follows:

- **Normal On** is the state that is visible when the object has been selected.
- **Normal Off** is the state that is visible when the form field has been deselected.
- **Rollover On** is the state that is visible when the mouse cursor moves over the form field when the field has been selected (the Normal On state).
- **Rollover Off** is the state that is visible when the mouse cursor moves over the form field when the field has not been selected (the Normal Off state).
- **Click On** is the state that is visible when the mouse button is pressed when the field has been selected (the Normal On state).
- **Click Off** is the state that is visible when the mouse button is pressed when the field has been deselected (the Normal Off state).

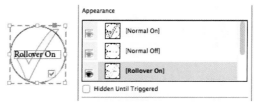

The Appearance area for check boxes and radio buttons contains separate On and Off states for Normal, Rollover, and Click.

You're not likely to need all the states for radio buttons and check boxes, but it's nice to know they're there if you do.

Checks and bullets

When you create a check box or a radio button, a default object is inserted into the button frame. This is a check mark for check boxes and a bullet for radio buttons. These are paths that can be selected and modified just like any path in InDesign.

The default check mark and bullet that are applied when you convert an object to a check box or radio button.

To modify the check mark or bullet, click once on the field. The dashed line appears, indicating that the form field itself is selected. Position the cursor over the check mark or bullet and click again. A regular frame appears around the object; this indicates that the path is selected. You can change the size, shape, fill, stroke, or effects applied to the path.

A form field that has been selected (left), and a path within the field that has been selected (right).

Once the check mark or bullet is selected, you can delete them from the field. You can then use the Place or Paste Into commands to add custom graphics to the form field. This makes your form more enjoyable.

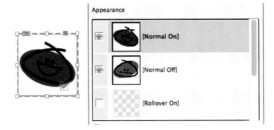

Using custom graphics for the Normal On and Normal Off states of a check box or radio button.

# Sample Buttons and Forms

In addition to creating your own buttons or forms, you can use the library of premade buttons and forms that Adobe has generously provided. The buttons already have Rollover states, as well as actions to go to pages and web addresses. There is even a navigation bar with four buttons that go to each page of a four-page document. The sample forms are sets of radio buttons, check boxes, and combo boxes with a variety of appearances.

TIP The sample buttons can be customized with new states, actions, and events, just like other buttons.

Using the Sample Buttons And Forms library

Choose Sample Buttons And Forms from the Buttons panel menu. The library panel opens. If you choose the Interactive for PDF workspace, the library panel also appears docked next to the other panels.

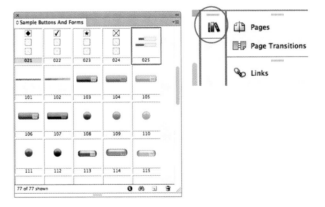

Choose Sample Buttons And Forms from the Buttons panel menu, or switch to the Interactive for PDF workspace, to access the Sample Buttons and Forms library panel.

Once you have the sample library open, you can easily add those buttons and forms to a document. Drag the item onto your document page, or select the item in the library and choose Place Item(s) from the panel menu.

There are four types of actions assigned to the sample buttons: Go To Page, Go To Next Page, Go To Previous Page, and Go To URL. There are three types of sample forms: check boxes, radio buttons, and combo boxes.

TIP All of the samples in the library are named, but they don't have descriptions. This is an opportunity for you to add descriptions that make it easier to find specific forms that you want to use.

Working with the buttons

The buttons in the library are pretty basic. They each have only one action. But they have very nicely designed Normal and Rollover states with 3D effects and drop shadows. We use them for more than the simple actions already applied.

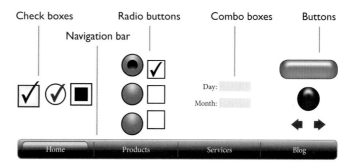

The types of buttons and forms in the Sample Buttons And Forms library panel.

Working with the check boxes

There are nine sample check boxes in the library. Each check box contains the artwork for at least one state: Normal On. However, not all the check boxes have artwork for the Normal Off state. And none of the sample check boxes contain artwork for any of the other states.

Some of the sample check boxes display a large check or cross for each state. Although they may look like the elements in a dingbat typeface, they are not a font—they are vector artwork that does not rely on a typeface.

The check boxes from the library all have a button value of "Yes." You need to change that entry for your own form data.

Working with the radio buttons

There are 13 sets of three radio buttons. While most people think of radio buttons as dots inside circles, the samples contain all sorts of artwork. Only two of the button sets contain artwork for all the states. The rest have artwork for only the Normal On and Normal Off states.

The radio button sets all have a value of "Choice." You can change that value for your own purposes. The Normal On state is selected by default for the top button in the set. The other two buttons have that option turned off.

Working with the combo box forms

We're delighted to see the set of two combo boxes included in the sample forms. These are labeled for days and months.

The form for the days of the month has a list of the numbers 1 through 31. This makes it easy to set up a form that can be used to pick a day of the month. The form for the months has a list of the numbers 1 through 12, which makes it easy to create a form that can be used for the months of the year. However, the months form does not have the names of the months. This is because every language version of InDesign uses the same library and English months would not be appropriate for foreign-language versions of the software.

# Animations

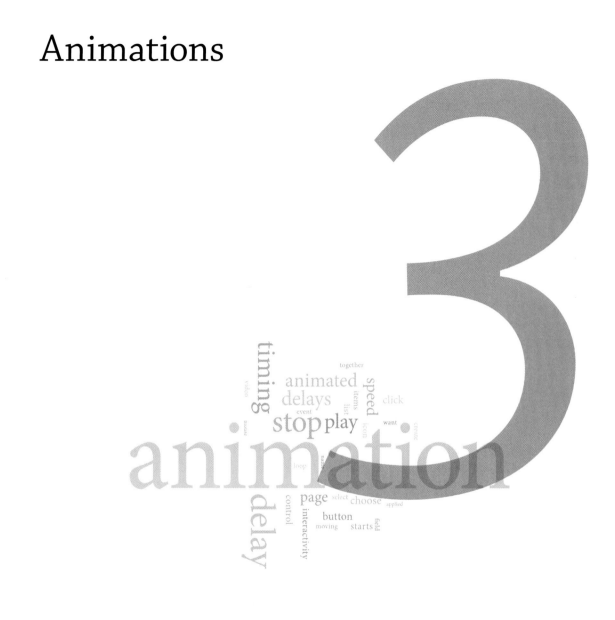

# In This Chapter

IT'S HARD TO FIND ANYONE UNDER **65** who didn't grow up watching cartoons on television. Kids have fun watching cartoon characters run, jump, and fly around the screen. It's the same creating animations for presentations and displays. Images and text can magically appear and disappear on the screen. Objects can jump up and down for emphasis. Illustrations can come to life.

Even if you've never created any sort of video or animation, it's easy to apply motion effects to InDesign elements. We like this much better than trying to work with Adobe Flash Professional. You use the familiar tools in InDesign but export SWF videos, which can then be incorporated into presentations and web graphics.

# Basic Animation Settings

Most of our favorite animations simply move a text frame or image onto a page. You can apply animations only to whole frames. You can't have just a single paragraph, such as a bullet point, move onto the page; each bullet point in the text would have to be in its own frame. However, as you will see, there are a wealth of ways to move objects around the page.

Objects can be animated to fade into view as they move onto a page.

## Exporting InDesign animations

The good news is that instead of having to go to Flash or some other animation program, you can animate the items on InDesign pages. The bad news is that exporting to SWF is the only way to use these animations. We wish there were more export options—especially for PDF and DPS.

However, before you give up using animations entirely, there are workarounds that let you use these animations as more than SWF files. We'll cover them in Chapter 7, "Exporting PDF and SWF."

Applying motion presets

The easiest way to animate objects is to use the animation presets that ship with InDesign. After you have applied a preset, you can then modify the actions of the animation. The primary controls for animations are applied using the Animation panel.

To open the Animation panel, choose Window > Interactive > Animation. Select the object or group that you want to animate. The object can be on or off the page.

TIP You can select more than one object to animate. However, the animation preset will be applied individually to each object. You can group the objects so they animate as a single object. This is not the same as having two separate objects animate together, which we'll cover on page 83.

The Animation panel and an object with the animation icon visible.

With the object selected, choose one of the animation presets from the **Preset** list. This applies an animation to the object, as indicated by the animation icon.

Most of the presets are well described by their names. For example, Fade-in applies the effect of the object fading into view. But the effect of a preset such as Pulse may not be immediately understood. You can preview its effect by applying the preset to the animated object. The picture of the butterfly in the Animation panel then animates according to that effect.

Naming the animation

When you apply a preset to an object, the object's **Name** field fills in with a generic description of the object. An empty rectangle frame is called *rectangle*. A text frame is named with the first few words of text. A graphics frame contains the name of the placed image. If you work with many animated objects, you will most likely want to change these generic names to something more explanatory.

Select the text in the Name field and replace it with a more descriptive name. We like to name animations with their appearance as well as the type of animation applied, such as "Flower moving from right."

The **Duration** field controls how long (in seconds) the animation plays. The motion presets apply a default setting that you may find too short. You can lengthen the animation by increasing this setting.

The **Speed** menu controls whether the animation accelerates or decelerates as it plays. Applying these settings makes the animation look more realistic. (Think of a car that starts, builds up speed, slows down, and then stops.) You can choose from the following options:

- **From Preset** uses the speed control that is applied by default to the animation preset.
- **None** keeps a constant speed throughout the animation. This is useful for animations that move in a single place, such as rotations.
- **Ease In** starts slowly and speeds up. This is most useful for animations where the object moves off the page.
- **Ease Out** starts at a constant speed and slows down at the end. This is most useful when the object starts off the page and then moves into view.
- **Ease In and Out** starts slowly, remains constant for a period of time, and then slows down. This is most useful when the object is visible throughout the duration of the animation.

Use the **Play** field to choose how many times the animation repeats. For most animations that move onto a page, you will want to set them to play only once. But for presets such as Gallop, which moves the object up and down, setting the Play field to more than 1 causes the object to jump several times.

Select **Loop** to repeat the animation endlessly. Setting an animation to endlessly play on a page is distracting. But that doesn't mean you can't loop objects such as the wheels on a car that moves across a page. The wheels should loop in that situation.

# Playing Animations

Animations are like movies on a page. They need some sort of prompt to start the show.

The **Events** list lets you choose which mouse or page actions trigger the animation. The default is to have the animation play when the page comes into view, or is loaded.

Choose a trigger option from the Events list. A check mark appears next to its name. You're not limited to just one event prompting an animation. For instance, you can have an animation play automatically when the page loads but also play when the viewer clicks the animated object. To add a second event for an animation, open the Events list again and choose another event. A second check mark appears next to that name. This indicates that two separate events can start the animation.

- **On Page Load** starts the animation when the page is visible. This can be when the viewer moves either forward or backward to view the page.
- **On Page Click** starts the animation when the user clicks anywhere on the page.
- **On Click (Self)** starts the animation when the object is clicked.
- **On Roll Over (Self)** starts the animation when the mouse moves over the area of the object.
- If you choose On Roll Over (Self), you can select **Reverse on Roll Off** to play the animation backwards when the mouse moves away from the object.

Creating a button to play an animation

You can also create a button to play an animation. The InDesign team figured (rightly) that people would want to quickly make buttons to play animated objects. So they made it very easy.

Start by applying a motion preset to the object. Then create the object that you want to use to trigger the animation. You don't have to turn this object into a button. That will happen automatically as you follow these steps.

Select the animation object, and then click the **Create Button Trigger** icon in the Animation panel. A tool tip instructs you to click the object that you want to start (trigger) the animation. This converts the object into a button and also applies the action to play the animation. You now have a button that will play the animation. You can also click a button that is already on the page to add playing the animation to the actions for that button.

---

TIP When you set a button to play an animation, On Button Event appears in the Events list for the animation, indicating that the animation can be triggered by a button.

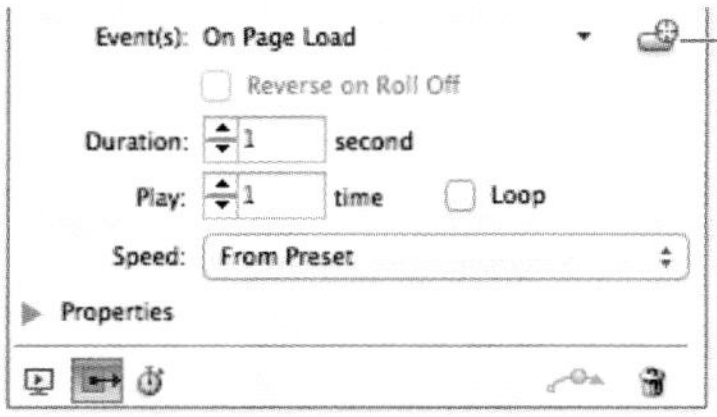

Create button trigger

Click the Create Button Trigger icon and then an object to convert that object into a button that plays the animation.

---

TIP The default event, Play on Page Load, will most likely still be applied to the animation. If you want only the button to prompt the animation, deselect Play on Page Load in the Events list.

---

# Animation Properties

The changes to the animation settings we've discussed so far are pretty basic. You can further refine animations by using the **Properties** controls in the Animation panel. (This part of the Animation panel is hidden by default; Adobe doesn't want to overwhelm you with options.) Click the Properties triangle (officially called a *twistie*) to open the Properties area of the Animation panel.

The Properties controls in the Animation panel.

Setting the animation appearance and location

You can customize how the animation starts or ends. From the Animate list, choose one of the following:

■ **From Current Appearance** uses the object's current position and appearance as the start of the animation. The object animates to match the properties set in the panel. This is the most common setting. It allows you to use the Properties panel to set the final appearance of the object.

**77**

An object set to animate From Current Appearance in the Properties area. Notice how the motion path indicates that the object will move to the right into a new position.

- **To Current Appearance** uses the object's current properties as the end of the animation. This allows you to set a specific end point for the animation; this setting is helpful when you want an object to animate onto a page but need the object to be visible when printing the page. If you don't select this setting, the object will be off the page when not animated.

Origin proxy box

An object set to animate To Current Appearance in the Properties area. Notice how the motion path indicates that the object will move to the left into its current position.

- **To Current Location** uses the object's current properties as the start of the animation and the object's position as the end of the animation. This option is similar to From Current Appearance, but the object finishes in its current location and the motion path is offset. Adobe recommends using this option for certain presets, such as blurs and fades, to prevent the object from appearing in an undesirable state at the end of the animation.

Setting the Rotate controls

Use the **Rotate** controls to specify the rotation degrees that the object completes during the animation.

Use the Origin proxy box to specify the origin point of the motion path on the animated object.

Scaling an object during an animation

Use the **Scale** fields to specify the percentage by which the object size increases or decreases during the animation. For instance, the Size animation preset increases the object size from 25% to 100%.

The default for this setting maintains a uniform scale for both horizontal and vertical scaling, but you can unlock the link setting to have the object scale disproportionally. We've created a very primitive animation of a bird flapping its wings by using a Scale setting that decreases horizontally only. Use the proxy box to choose at which point on the object the scaling will occur. Our bird scales from its center.

A simple horizontal scale can create the effect of a bird flapping its wings.

Setting the opacity for an animation

There are two animation presets, Fade In and Fade Out, that set an object to slowly appear or disappear on the page. But what if you want the object to appear or disappear as part of a move across the page? The **Opacity** menu is a separate setting that can be applied as part of other animation presets. Choose one of the following from the Opacity list:

- **None** uses no opacity setting, so there is no change in the visibility of the object.
- **Fade In** causes the object to gradually become visible.
- **Fade Out** causes the object to gradually become invisible.

Setting the Visibility options

You may want to control whether an object is visible before it starts its animation or remains visible on the page after it finishes its animation. These settings are very useful when you want multiple objects to follow the same animation path but disappear to let the next object be seen. There are two visibility options:

- **Hide Until Animated** keeps the object invisible until it starts the animation.
- **Hide After Animating** makes the object invisible after it finishes the animation.

Using the animation proxy

Without actual motion on the page, it can be difficult to imagine how the animation will appear. The animation proxy is a gray shadow that shows where the actual object will move from or to as part of the animation. Turning on the animation proxy creates a gray box or outline of the shape that indicates the start or end of the animation.

The gray animation proxy helps you see how the actual animation will appear.

Click the **Show Animation Proxy** button in the Animation panel so it is highlighted. This turns on the display of the animation proxy. Click again to hide the proxy.

Show Animation Proxy

Click the Show Animation Proxy button to display a gray shadow that shows the first or final position of an object along a motion path.

Saving custom settings

Most likely, you're going to spend time customizing the motion presets. If you have put in all that time and hard work, you will want to save the preset for future work.

With the object selected, choose Save from the Animation panel menu. This opens the Save Preset dialog box. Name the preset and click OK. The custom preset appears in the Preset list in the Animation panel for all InDesign documents.

# Motion Paths

When you apply an animation that involves motion, a green motion preset line appears when you click the object with the Selection tool. This line controls the position and direction of the object's motion. A circle indicates the starting position of the animation; an arrow indicates the direction and the ending position. You can edit this motion preset line to customize the move. For instance, you can lengthen the line to have the object move along a longer path.

Most of the preset motion paths are straight lines. To create a more natural effect, we like to add curves to these paths so they move slightly up or down into position.

Editing the motion path

Select the animated object. The motion preset line appears as a green line. An arrow indicates the direction of the animation.

The green line indicates the direction and length of the object's path.

Click the motion preset line. The line changes from a motion path to a regular InDesign path. Use the Direct Selection tool to modify the points on the path. Use the Pen tool, the Pencil tool, or the Smooth tool to add, delete, or modify the points on the path. Deselect the object to apply the changes.

**Creating a custom motion path**

Instead of modifying the built-in motion paths, you can draw your own motion paths for an animated object. Start by using the Pen tool or the Line tool to draw the open path that you want to use as a motion path. Select both the path and the object you want to animate. Click the **Convert to Motion Path** icon in the Animation panel. This converts the path into a motion path and opens the animation controls for the object.

You can also swap an external motion path for one already applied to an animation object. Select both the open path and the animation object. Click the Convert to Motion Path icon. The new path is applied as the motion path to the animation. The original motion path is deleted.

Convert to Motion Path

The Convert to Motion Path icon allows you to use your own paths as the motion paths for animations.

**Importing presets from Flash**

In addition to creating animation presets in InDesign, you can export a preset from Adobe Flash and then import it into InDesign. These effects can be much more sophisticated than those created in InDesign.

TIP The presets that ship with InDesign are actually the same as the default Flash presets. Use this technique to import the new presets you create in Flash.

In Flash, select a motion preset and choose Export from the Motion Preset panel. Name the XML file.

In InDesign, choose **Manage Presets** from the Animation panel to open the Manage Presets dialog box. Click the Load button and navigate to the XML file you previously saved. Click OK. The preset is added to the InDesign Preset menu.

TIP You can also use the Manage Presets dialog box to duplicate or delete presets.

| Manage Presets | |
|---|---|
| Appear on a path | **Done** |
| Swoosh around the page | |
| [Appear] | Delete |
| [Bounce Right (large)] | |
| [Bounce Right (medium)] | Duplicate |
| [Bounce Right (small)] | |
| [Bounce Vertical] | Load... |
| [Bounce and Smoosh] | |
| [Dance] | Save As... |
| [Disappear] | |

The Manage Presets dialog box allows you to import and work with custom presets. Your own saved presets appear at the top of the list.

Removing animations

If you no longer want an object to be animated, you can convert it back into an ordinary object. Select the animated object, and in the Animation panel click the **Remove Animation** icon.

Remove Animation

The Remove Animation icon converts an animated object into an ordinary object.

# Timing

Just as in comedy, when working with animation, timing is everything. So in addition to the duration controls in the Animation panel, you can use the Timing panel to control how an animation plays. The Timing panel has three important features. The first allows you to delay the start of an animation. The second changes the order in which objects are animated. The third causes animations on different objects to start at the same time.

Setting the delay for animated objects

Open the Timing panel (Window > Interactive > Timing). All the animated objects for that spread are listed.

TIP You don't add items to the Timing panel. They appear automatically when you create animated objects.

The Timing panel lets you refine how animations play.

In the Timing panel, not on the page itself, click the name of the object you want to control. Use the **Delay** field to set the length of time (in seconds) that the object's animation will be delayed.

Your animation may be triggered by more than one event, such as On Page Load as well as On Button Event. You can set different delays for each event. For instance, you might want a slight delay after the page loads to give the user a moment to get accustomed to the look of the page before the start of the animation. But you might want no delay if the user clicks a button to start the animation, assuming that the user will want a prompt response to his or her action.

Changing the order in which objects are animated

The Timing panel also lets you control the order in which objects are animated. Drag the name of the object up or down in the list in the Timing panel. Objects are played from the top of the list down, and are added to the panel in the order in which you create them on the spread.

Playing objects together

Each object in the Timing panel plays individually. However, you can link objects so they play at the same time. This is very helpful when you have two objects with separate motion paths or presets that you want to animate together.

Select the names of the objects in the Timing panel. Click the **Play Together** icon in the Timing panel. A bracket appears around the selected items, indicating that they will play together.

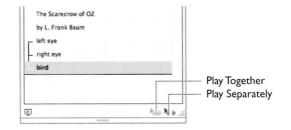

Use the Play Together icon to set separate animations to play at the same time. Brackets indicate that those objects that will play together.

If you have items linked to play together, you can use the Play field and the Loop control to control how many times they play.

TIP Click the Play Separately icon to release the items from playing together.

## Timing is everything!

Even the slightest change in timing can make an enormous difference in the effectiveness of an animation. While we can't anticipate every timing situation, here are some general rules we try to follow:

**Take a moment:** When items are set to play on the loading of a page, you may want to set a slight delay before they play. This gives your viewers a moment to get accustomed to the appearance of the page.

**Up the pacing:** Nothing is more boring than elements that move too slowly onto the page. This means that the speed of the animation, as set in the Animation panel as well as the Timing panel, should be short. Your audience can anticipate where an object is moving, so don't bore them by making them watch it happen.

**Overlap events:** Start the next animation just a moment before the previous object settles into place or finishes a fade. Your viewers have already digested the motion of the first object and are eagerly anticipating the next.

# Previewing Animations

Applying motion presets and modifying animations may feel like working in the dark, because animated objects don't move around the InDesign page. So you may feel a little lost as to whether or not the settings are working properly. Use the SWF Preview panel to see if your animations are set correctly.

TIP You can also use the SWF Preview panel to preview interactive and multimedia elements such as buttons, movies, and hyperlinks (covered in Chapter 2). However, the SWF Preview panel doesn't preview PDF-only interactivity such as filling in forms or certain button actions. When you want to preview PDF interactivity, you need to open the PDF in Acrobat.

Using the SWF Preview panel

Choose Window > Interactive > SWF Preview to open the SWF Preview panel. The default size of the panel is much too small! Drag the corners or edges of the panel to increase the size of the preview area. This makes it easier to view animations and click interactive items.

The SWF Preview panel lets you preview animations as well as interactive and multimedia elements.

Click one of the preview selection mode buttons:

- **Preview Selection mode** sets the SWF Preview panel to display only the selected object. Use this when you have many interactive elements on a page and need to test just one or two elements. This helps the preview play faster.
- **Preview Page mode** sets the SWF Preview panel to display the currently selected spread. Use this when you need to preview a single spread.
- **Preview Document mode** sets the SWF Preview panel to display the entire document.

TIP You'll probably want to preview your work constantly as you create animations. You'll work faster if you use keyboard shortcuts. To preview the current spread, hold the keyboard shortcut Cmd/Ctrl-Shift and press the Return/Enter key. To preview the entire document, hold Cmd-Shift-Opt (Mac) or (Ctrl-Shift-Alt) (Windows) and press the Return/Enter key.

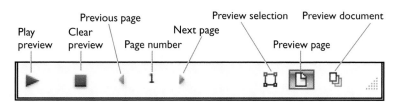

The SWF Preview panel controls.

Click the **Play Preview** button to display the page with the animation objects. If there are any animations set to play on page load, they will play automatically.

If you edit the document, use the Clear Preview button to delete the previous version of the document from the SWF Preview panel. Then click the Play Preview button again to see the new version of the page.

Use the **Go to Next Page** and **Go to Previous Page** buttons to move through the document.

Move your mouse over the preview area of the SWF Preview panel and click your animated objects. Interactive elements react to the mouse as they would in an exported SWF.

The SWF Preview panel displays the interactive elements as they would appear using the current settings in the SWF Export dialog. Conversely, if you change settings in the SWF Preview panel, these changes are reflected in the SWF Export dialog box.

**To edit the SWF Preview panel settings**

Choose Edit Preview Settings from the SWF Preview panel menu. The Preview Settings dialog box appears.

TIP This dialog box is the same as the Export SWF dialog box. For details on these settings, see "Setting the General SWF options" on page 239 and "Setting the Advanced SWF options" on page 242.

Make whatever adjustments you want in the Preview Settings dialog box. Click Save Settings to apply the changes to the SWF Preview panel.

**To test the export in a browser**

While the SWF Preview panel is very good at showing the interactivity on your page, you also need to test the files in an actual browser. Rather than littering your hard disk with test files, you can use the **Test in Browser** command.

Choose Test in Browser from the SWF Preview panel menu. The file opens in your computer's default browser. The animation automatically plays. If you want to test the file in a different browser, you need to change the default browser using your computer's controls. On the Mac, you change the browser by changing the preferences in Safari. On Windows, use the Control panel Default Programs to associate the new browser with web files.

TIP You need to have the Flash Player installed in order to preview in a browser.

**To use the SWF Preview panel from other panels**

Once you start refining animations, you'll want to preview the results. The InDesign team has made it more convenient to invoke the SWF Preview panel command by adding Preview icons at the bottom of the Animation panel, the Buttons panel, and the Timing panel. Click the Preview icon at the bottom of those panels to open the SWF Preview panel.

Preview

Look for the Preview icon in the Animation panel, the Buttons panel, or the Timing panel.

**TIP** These icons are faster than using the Play button in the SWF Preview panel because they automatically clear the preview and set it to play.

# Layout Controls

# In This Chapter

UNLIKE PRINT BOOKS AND MAGAZINES, which tend to have a constant page size from one copy to another, digital publications can morph from one size to another depending on the device the reader is using.

Consider the different sizes of iPads, Kindle Fires, Nooks, Android tablets, and smartphones. Each one needs its own layout size. To add to those sizes, those devices may allow the reader to rotate the device from vertical to horizontal layout. Suddenly there are quite a number of different layout sizes and orientations to handle. This is where the layout tools for working with page sizes and designs come into play. Fortunately, they're also helpful for the occasional print layouts that change size.

*Alternate Layout* is a set of commands that means that one document can have several different page sizes and orientations within the file. It also means that elements from one layout are linked to elements in the other layouts. So if you change the text on the vertical layout, it updates on the horizontal one.

*Liquid Layout* is an intelligence that you can specify for a page. It causes the elements on that page to automatically change their shape and/or move into new positions to fit the new layout when you change the size and orientation of the InDesign page.

You also can use various tools and commands to further control how text and images are modified as their frames change size and orientation. These are *Auto-Fit* options for images, *Auto-Size* for text frames, and *Flexible Width* for columns.

# Setting Page Sizes

When you design for print, you need to know the size of the paper your document will be printed on. Similarly, when you design for digital publications, you need to know the size of the device that your document will be viewed on. This isn't as simple as working in print.

The "page size" (size of the screen) is different for the iPad versus the Kindle Fire or the Android devices. You need to know which device your application is going to be used on and set the screen size accordingly.

Finding tablet and smartphone sizes

Most manufacturers list two different sizes for their devices. The *device size* is the size of the entire tablet, including the frame and any hardware around the screen. The *screen dimensions* are the number of pixels of the actual area of the screen. The manufacturer will often also list the *resolution* of the device. Just as with a computer screen, the higher the resolution, the more detail there is on the device screen. You need to enter the screen dimensions when designing digital publications.

When you create tablet applications for the iPad or for Android devices, you will want to create individual page sizes for the various screen dimensions of those devices. (*We cover the details of creating DPS apps in Chapter 5, "Tablet Applications."*)

Fortunately, Adobe ships InDesign with page sizes for some common tablets. When you choose Digital Publishing from the Intent menu in the New Document dialog box, the Page Size menu displays the sizes, in pixels, for the iPhone, iPad, Kindle Fire/Nook, and Android 10" devices. The Android 10" label denotes tablets from many different manufacturers that all use the same Android operating system and screen dimensions.

The Page Size menu of the New Document dialog box shows a few of the most common devices for digital publishing.

These are the dimensions of the four default tablet sizes in the New Document dialog box:

| Device | Dimensions | Resolution |
| --- | --- | --- |
| **iPhone** | 960 x 640 pixels | 326 ppi |
| **iPad** | 1024 x 768 pixels | 132 ppi |
| **Kindle Fire/Nook** | 1024 x 600 pixels | 169 ppi |

| Device | Dimensions | Resolution |
| --- | --- | --- |
| **Android 10"** | 1280 x 800 | 149 ppi |

TIP It's highly possible that by the time this book is printed there will be new tablets on the market with different screen dimensions. Go to the manufacturer's website to get the size of the specific device you're designing for.

Understanding resolution

The glass screen of an iPhone 4S is 3.5 inches (diagonal). The glass screen of an iPad is 9.5 inches (diagonal). The iPad's screen is almost three times bigger than the iPhone's screen. But the screen dimensions of the iPhone are about 80 percent of the iPad's dimensions. How can something one-third the size be almost the same screen dimensions?

The answer is that the original iPad and the iPad 2 have a resolution of 132 ppi, while the iPhone has a much denser resolution of 326 ppi. This means that while the iPad has a larger screen, there is more detail available for zooming on the iPhone.

Apple recently came out with a new iPad. The glass screen of this new iPad (2012) is exactly the same size as the screen of the iPad 2. But the screen dimensions of the iPad (2012) are 2048 x 1536 — twice the size of the iPad 2. This is because the resolution of the iPad (2012) is 264 — twice the resolution of the iPad 2. So how should you design one application for the two different iPads?

Fortunately, you don't have to worry about designing for the two different types of iPad screens. As long as the aspect ratios are the same — and they are — you can design for the original iPad screen and its lower resolution.

Understanding aspect ratio

When you are designing for digital devices, it helps to know the *aspect ratio* of the device. This is the relationship of one side to another. This is very important if you want to modify a layout to be used on a different device.

The greater the difference in the aspect ratio, the longer one side will be than the other. For instance, if the aspect ration is 1:1, then the screen is a square. The aspect ratio for the iPad is 4:3. This is close to a square, but one side is slightly longer than the other. 4:3 is similar to the aspect ratio of a standard television screen.

The aspect ratio for the Fire and the Nook is 16:9. This means that one side is much longer than the other. This aspect ratio happens to be the one used by widescreen television shows. So those videos fit the screen of a Fire better than they do an iPad.

So what happens if you design an application for one device and then port it over to a tablet with a different aspect ratio? The application will shrink or expand to fit the new screen area. But since the new screen has a different aspect ratio, there will be empty space around the application.

You're probably familiar with this effect from watching television. When a TV show that was shot in the widescreen format is shown on a widescreen television, the image fits perfectly. But if a movie or show has a different aspect ratio from the television, black bands are added to the outside of the image area.

The same thing happens when magazines or apps that are designed for just one aspect ratio and are ported over to a device with a different aspect ratio. There will be empty space on the outside of the image. This is the important reason why you need different designs for the various aspect ratios of devices.

A comparison of the aspect ratios of three tablet devices playing a widescreen television show. The video fits perfectly on a Fire or a Nook. The iPad has noticeable letterboxing bands. But the letterboxing on the Xoom is less noticeable because its aspect ratio is closer to the aspect ratio for a widescreen show.

**Setting and saving custom page sizes**

If your device is not listed in the New Document dialog box, use the Height and Width fields to enter its dimensions in pixels. (The unit of measurement automatically changes to pixels when you choose the Digital Publishing intent.)

TIP You don't have to calculate the aspect ratio for a specific screen size. As soon as you enter the screen dimensions, you have automatically set the correct aspect ratio.

As new tablets enter the market, you will most likely want to save those sizes as custom pages. Enter the width and height measurements, and then choose **Custom** from the Page Size menu. This opens the Custom Page Size dialog box, where you can name the custom page. In addition to creating page sizes for new devices, you may also want to create custom page sizes for the horizontal or vertical orientations. That way, you won't have to click the orientation icons to change from horizontal to vertical pages.

TIP Deselect Facing Pages when creating layouts for digital publications. There are no left- or right-hand pages on a screen.

```
                    Custom Page Size
    Name:  Microsoft Surface                 OK

   Width:  ⇕ 1366 px          🔲 🔳        Cancel
  Height:  ⇕ 768 px

          ┌──────────────────────┐          Add
          │                      │
          │                      │         Delete
          │                      │
          │                      │
          │                      │
          │                      │
          └──────────────────────┘
```

The Custom Page Size dialog box lets you define and store screen dimensions for devices that are not listed in the New Document dialog box.

# Working with Alternate Layouts

The ability to create different-sized pages within a single InDesign document was introduced in InDesign CS5. It was, however, a bit of a hassle to quickly create new sets of pages with a different layout size and orientation. With the Alternate Layout feature, introduced in CS6, you have easier ways of creating the new page sizes as well as managing the layouts in the Pages panel.

*Setting up the Pages panel*

There are three different views for the Pages panel: **Horizontally**, **Vertically**, and **By Alternate Layout**. The Horizontally and Vertically settings are used primarily for print layouts. By Alternate Layout is used for working with digital publications. It allows you to see the alternate layouts in the document side by side in the Pages panel.

When you choose Digital Publishing from the Intent menu for a document, the Pages panel is automatically set to the By Alternate Layout display. The panel is also changed to By Alternate Layout when you choose Digital Publishing from the Workspace menu. Or you can change the setting by going to the Pages panel menu and choosing View Pages > By Alternate Layout.

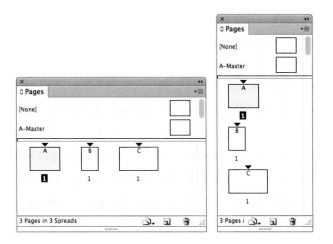

The Pages panel, set to View Horizontally (left) and View Vertically (right). Although the different-sized pages are shown, these settings do not label the alternate layouts with the devices they are being designed for.

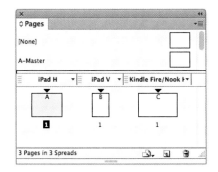

The Pages panel, set to View By Alternate Layout, labels the different layouts within the document. Notice that the page displays for the alternate layout pages have different sizes, orientations, and aspect ratios.

TIP If you have a document set for a Print or Web intent, the Pages panel automatically switches to View By Alternate Layout when you add an alternate layout to the document.

To create an alternate layout

To create an alternate layout, choose Create Alternate Layout from the Pages panel menu or the Layout menu. This opens the Create Alternate Layout dialog box.

Rather than cover the options for this dialog box all at once, we'll divide them up into sections.

```
┌─────────────────────────────────────────────────────┐
│              Create Alternate Layout                 │
│                                                       │
│              Name:  iPad V                             │
│   From Source Pages:  iPad H                    ⬍     │
│  ┌─Page Size:  iPad                      ⬍──────────┐ │
│  │                                                   │ │
│  │   Width: ⬍ 768 px        Orientation: 🔲 🔳     │ │
│  │   Height: ⬍ 1024 px                              │ │
│  └───────────────────────────────────────────────── │
│  ┌─Options──────────────────────────────────────────┐│
│  │  Liquid Page Rule:  Preserve Existing      ⬍     ││
│  │  ☑ Link Stories                                  ││
│  │  ☑ Copy Text Styles to New Style Group           ││
│  │  ☑ Smart Text Reflow                             ││
│  └───────────────────────────────────────────────────┘│
│                              Cancel      ┌──  OK  ──┐ │
└─────────────────────────────────────────────────────┘
```

The Create Alternate Layout dialog box lets you set the options for new layouts added to the document.

**To set the name and source page**

Use the **Name** field to enter a name for the alternate layout. By default, the alternate layout is named from the source pages with a change in the orientation. So if you have been working on a horizontal iPad layout, the default name for the alternate layout is "iPad V."

TIP InDesign recognizes the orientation of the alternate layout and adds a V (for vertical) or an H (for horizontal) after the name.

Use the **Page Size** menu to choose one of the preset page sizes. These are the same choices that were available in the New Document dialog box.

If you want to enter your own sizes, use the **Width** and **Height** controls to apply custom dimensions to the alternate layout. Click the horizontal or vertical icons to flip the orientation of the alternate layout.

**Using the Liquid Layout menu**

When you create an alternate layout, you will want to set how objects on the page are resized and repositioned. This is where Liquid Layout rules come into play. You use the Liquid Layout Rule menu to set how the items and text will be modified to fit the alternate layout. (*See the next section, "Using Liquid Layout Rules."*)

TIP Unless you choose Preserve Existing, the Liquid Page Rule setting in the Create Alternate Layout dialog box overrides the settings applied to the individual pages.

**Linking text between alternate layouts**

When you create an alternate layout, the text and images from the source layout are duplicated in the alternate layouts. What happens, though, if you make changes to the text in one layout? You wouldn't want to have to go through each of the alternate layouts to make those changes. Select the **Link Stories** check box so that changes to text in the source layout

**97**

are applied to the stories in the alternate layout. (*See the section "Linking Items" for more information on using this feature.*)

Managing text styles

Select the **Copy Text Styles to New Style Group** check box to take the styles from the source document and make duplicates of them in the Paragraph Styles panel. This command collects all the styles from the original layout and puts them in a second style group folder labeled with the alternate layout name. It also applies the styles in the second style group to the alternate layout text. (*For more information on copying styles between alternate layouts, see the section "Linking Styles" on page 111.*)

Setting the other Alternate Layout options

Select the **Smart Text Reflow** check box to automatically add pages to the alternate layout if an overset is created. This is very helpful if you have a layout with long text.

TIP This is the same as turning on Smart Text Reflow in Preferences > Type Preferences.

Using alternate layout master pages

As you create each new alternate layout, a new master page is added for that alternate layout. The pages created by the alternate layout are automatically based on the new master.

If you need to change the size of the alternate layout pages, you should not select the document pages. Instead, select the master page with the Page tool and change the page size there.

TIP The Document Size dialog box will change the size for only the first layout in the document, not for the alternate layouts.

# Using Liquid Layout Rules

When you create alternate layouts, you'll often need to adjust the size and shape of the elements to fit the size of the new pages. Liquid Layout rules are electronic settings that control how these elements change. Liquid Layout rules help automate the process of producing alternate layouts, but each page will likely require some adjusting afterwards.

Applying Liquid Layout rules

Choose the Page tool from the Tools panel. If the page is not automatically selected, click the page to which you want to apply a Liquid Layout rule. You can click the actual page with the Page tool, or you can click the page icon in the Pages panel. You can also use the Pages panel to select more than one page at a time.

TIP You cannot combine several Liquid Layout rules on the same page. Each page can have only one Liquid Layout rule applied to it.

Use the Liquid Layout area in the Control panel to choose a Liquid Layout rule for the page.

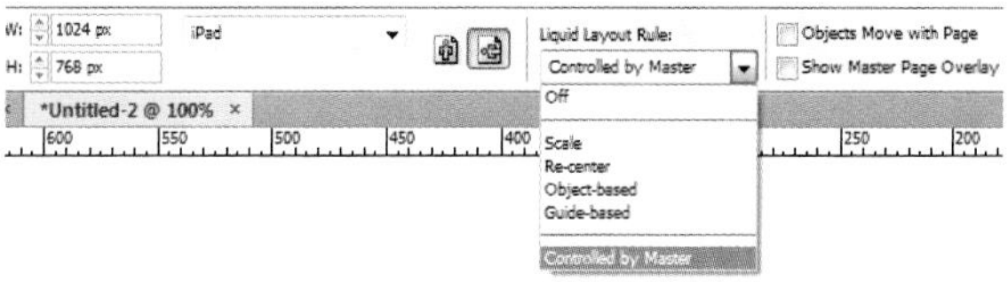

When the Page tool is active, the Control panel displays the Liquid Layout Rule menu.

TIP You can also use the Liquid Layout panel to set Liquid Layout rules. Choose Layout > Liquid Layout to open the panel.

These Liquid Layout rules are explained in the following chart.

| Liquid Layout Rule | Description | Comments |
| --- | --- | --- |
| **Off** | Turns off the Liquid Layout rules for the page. Objects do not change their size or shape. | |
| **Scale** | Objects are scaled as the page changes. Text and images are scaled to fit within the new frame size and shape. | This is the only rule that scales text and images. |
| **Re-center** | Objects do not resize but are kept in the center of the page. Whitespace is added around the objects. | No whitespace is added, and images are not affected if the page size is made smaller. |
| **Object-based** | Allows you to set whether the width or height of the object should change. Also allows you to maintain the relative space between the object's sides and the sides of the page. | Requires individual settings for each object. |
| **Guide-based** | Uses guides to set whether an object's width or height should change. The position of the guides controls which objects are affected. | Requires slightly less work than the Object-based rule. |
| **Controlled by Master** | Uses the setting that has been applied to the master page governing the page. | Allows you to quickly apply a Liquid Layout rule to multiple pages in the layout. |
| **Preserve Existing** | Uses the setting that has been applied to each page. | Is available only in the Create Alternate Layout dialog box. |

## How much to expect from Liquid Layout adjustments

It is very tempting to expect that Liquid Layout rules will completely automate the process of creating an alternate layout. With just a click of the mouse, elements would resize, reshape, and rescale to create a perfect new layout.

Sadly, that is not the case. Even a simple layout with a few basic elements won't necessarily translate perfectly when the alternate layout is created with a particular Liquid Layout rule.

Think of the Liquid Layout feature as the starting point for converting one layout into another. But don't be disappointed if you need to tweak one or two elements in the new layout.

**Using the Scale rule**

The **Scale** rule is the easiest to apply and understand. When the Scale rule is applied to a layout, the objects shrink or expand to fit in the new page size and shape. This is similar to grouping the elements on a page and dragging with the Free Transform tool. Text point sizes change, as well as the size of images within frames.

Let's say you start with a vertical layout for the iPad. The size of the page is 768 x 1024. You then use the Scale rule to create an alternate layout for the vertical layout of the Fire/Nook. This page is 600 x 1024. The height of the page remains constant, but the width needs to shrink.

When the Scale rule is applied, the objects scale down to fit the new width, but that leaves a lot of whitespace at the top and bottom of the page. The Scale rule gives the best results when the source page and the new layout have aspect ratios that are identical or very similar.

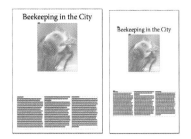

An example of how the Scale rule changes the size of objects from the iPad to the Fire/Nook. Notice that the point size of the text as well as the size of the image are reduced to fit the smaller width. Notice also that there is whitespace added at the top and bottom of the layout.

**Using the Re-center rule**

The **Re-center** rule adds or removes space for the new page size without changing the size of the elements on the page. As space is added to the page, the objects are repositioned so they stay centered on the page.

This rule creates satisfactory results if the page increases in size. But if the page is made smaller, you need to set the objects far enough from the edges of the page so that they don't get cropped as the page edges move inward.

An example of what happens when the Re-center rule is applied to change a layout from iPad H to iPad V. Notice that the elements are centered horizontally on the page. But they extend vertically off the page because the Re-center rule does not change the size or shape of the elements.

Using the Guide-based rule

The **Guide-based** Liquid Layout rule uses guides to designate which objects on the page should resize and in what direction. These are special guides called Liquid guides.

To create a Liquid guide, switch to the Page tool and use the Page tool cursor to drag a guide out from the horizontal or vertical ruler. The Liquid guide appears. Liquid guides are indicated on the page by dashed lines (rather than the solid lines of Ruler guides). When selected, a Liquid guide displays a special icon ⊞ that distinguishes it from a Ruler guide ⊞. Click the icon to turn a Ruler guide into a Liquid guide and vice versa.

Liquid guides control the objects they touch on the page. Vertical Liquid guides allow the object to expand or contract from left to right. Horizontal Liquid guides allow the object to expand or contract from top to bottom.

Position the Liquid guide so that it crosses the items on the page that you want to resize. The Liquid guide does not have to cross through the center of an object; it only has to move through the object.

TIP Liquid guides can also be placed on the master for document pages. This makes it much simpler to apply the Guide-based rule to multiple pages.

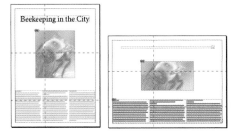

An example of how the Guide-based Liquid Layout rule changes objects from one orientation to another. In this case, the bottom text and image are set to change both their height and width, but the top text adjusts only horizontally.

Using the Object-based rule

The **Object-based** rule provides the most control over how items change as the page size changes, but it is also the most complex. Unlike the Guide-based rule, which controls only the height and width of an object, the Object-based rule lets you apply six adjustments to the shape of an object.

With the Page tool selected, choose Object-based from the Liquid Layout Rule menu in the Control panel. Then click the object that you want to control. The object-based controllers appear over the item.

On the top, bottom, left, and right sides of the object are the controls that govern whether the space between the edge of the page and the edge of the object is flexible or pinned. Set the edge to be flexible if you want the space between the object and the page edge to adjust. Set the edge to be pinned to maintain the relative spacing between the object and the page edge.

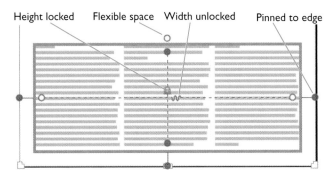

The object-based controls.

The edge controls let you keep an object in a specific area on the page. For instance, if you pin the bottom edge controller to the page, that edge of the object will maintain its position relative to the bottom edge of the page.

Inside the object are the controllers to set whether the width or height of the object adjusts. A spring icon indicates that the height or width can change as the page size changes. A lock icon indicates that the height or width is fixed.

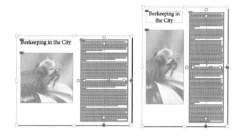

An example of how the Object-based Liquid Layout rule controls the change from one layout to another. In this case, the right-hand text frame is pinned to the bottom and right edges of the page. This allows the frame to adjust its height and width while still hugging the page edges.

The controls need to be applied to each object on the page, but instead of manually setting them for each object, you can apply the controls to objects on the master page. Those settings are then applied to the master page objects on the document page. If there are objects on the page that are not controlled by the master, you need to set those controls on the document page.

TIP You can set only two out of the three settings on each axis. For instance, if you pin the left and right edges to the page, then the width of the object has to be unlocked. If the height and top edge are locked and pinned, then the bottom edge has to remain flexible.

**Using the Liquid Layout panel**

As an alternative to setting the Liquid Layout rules using the Control panel, you can use the Liquid Layout panel. Choose Layout > Liquid Layout to open the panel. You can then choose a Liquid Layout rule. If you choose Object-based, you will see check boxes for Resize with Page and Pin. These are the same controls as the ones that appear over the object. You can set them as you want.

**Tips for using Liquid Layout rules**

Liquid Layout is a sophisticated feature, and setting the rules requires a certain amount of experimentation. Here are a few techniques we suggest for getting a handle on Liquid Layout rules.

- After you set a Liquid Layout rule to the page, resize the page by dragging one of the handles on the page with the Page tool. Watch how the objects resize and reposition. This will give you a better idea of how the Liquid Layout rule will affect the page. When you release the drag, the page snaps back to its original dimensions. Hold the Opt/Alt key as you drag if you don't want the page to snap back to its original dimension when you release the drag.

- Crop images so there is extra image outside the frame. If the image frame expands, this ensures that there is more of the image to be displayed.
- Choose Flexible Width from the Column menu (*covered on page 117*) so that text frames automatically add or delete columns as the page width increases or decreases.
- Use the Auto-Size settings for text frames (*covered on page 116*) so that the text frames expand or contract to fit the text.
- Use the Auto-Fit Content Fitting options for image frames (*covered on page 115*) to control how images expand or contract as the frame adjusts.

The Liquid Layout panel contains check boxes that allow you to set the controllers for an Object-based Liquid Layout rule.

**Using Layout Adjustment** Liquid Layout is not the only technique for adjusting page items when you change pages sizes. Earlier versions of InDesign have a feature called Layout Adjustment. This is a very primitive technique compared to Liquid Layout, but some people are more comfortable with the simple controls of Layout Adjustment. If you work with layouts created in versions of InDesign before CS6, it's possible that Layout Adjustment will be turned on.

Layout Adjustment conflicts with Liquid Layout. You can't have both applied. To turn off Layout Adjustment, open the Liquid Layout panel. In the panel menu, deselect the Layout Adjustment check box. This lets you work with the Liquid Layout feature.

# Using the Content Tools

When you create an alternate layout, elements from one page are automatically copied onto another. You can also manually copy elements from one page or document to another using the Content tools — the **Content Collector**, **Content Placer**, and **Content Conveyor**. These give you more control over how objects are placed and linked.

Content Collector   Content Placer   Content Conveyor

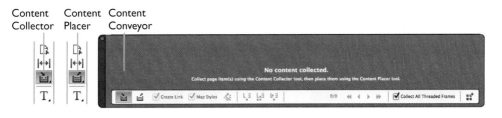

The Content tools.

**To collect content**

Choose the **Content Collector** tool from the Tools panel. The Content Conveyor automatically appears. Unless you have previously collected content, the Content Conveyor is empty.

Click to select the item that you want to place elsewhere. A preview of each item appears in the Content Conveyor as it is selected. Click to continue to collect other items. Each item appears in the Content Conveyor.

You can also drag with the Content Collector to select multiple items. This creates a set. A number appears next to the preview in the Content Collector cursor, indicating how many items are in the set. All the items in a set are placed together on the page.

Number of items in set                    Last item in queue

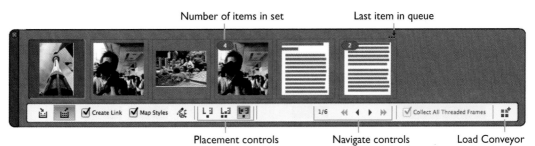

Placement controls          Navigate controls          Load Conveyor

The Content Conveyor as it appears with collected items.

TIP If you want to hide the Content Conveyor but still use the Content tools, press Opt/Alt-B. Press the keystroke again to reshow the Content Conveyor.

**To place content**

Once you have collected content, you can place it in a different area of the page, on a different page, or even on a different document. The **Content Placer** is nested with the Content Collector in the Tools panel. You can also choose it from the Content Conveyor. But our favorite way to select the two tools is to tap the B key; this toggles between the two tools.

Move to the new area, page, or document where you want the content to be placed. A preview of the content appears in the cursor. If there is more than one item in the Content Conveyor, a number appears in the cursor preview, indicating how many items are in the Content Conveyor.

The Content Placer cursor with a preview of the placed item.

Click or drag to place the item. If you click, you place the item at the same size as its source. If you drag, the size of the area determines the size of the placed item. Dragged items are automatically constrained to the same proportions as the source. Hold the Shift key to change the proportions of the placed objects.

TIP You can quickly place items using the Edit > Place and Link command. This loads the item into the Content Conveyor and switches to the Content Placer tool.

As you place content, the Content Conveyor highlights the next item in the queue for placing. You can skip an item by using the left and right arrow keys on your keyboard or the Previous and Next controls in the Content Conveyor. Click the escape (esc) key on the keyboard to delete an item from the Content Conveyor.

TIP Items remain in the Content Conveyor until it is emptied or until you quit that session of InDesign.

To control the placement of items

You can control whether items in the Content Conveyor are kept or deleted as they are placed. This is helpful for those times you want to keep items for placement elsewhere.

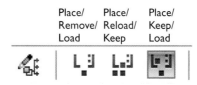

The Content Conveyor controls for how items are placed, removed, reloaded, and kept.

With the Content Placer selected, choose one of the following controls from the Content Conveyor:

- **Place/Remove/Load** places the content, removes it from the Content Conveyor, and then loads the next item. Use this setting when you want to place an item once and then delete it from the Content Conveyor.

- **Place/Reload/Keep** places the content on the page, keeps it in the Content Conveyor, and then reloads it for placement again. This is helpful if you want to keep placing the same item over and over.
- **Place/Keep/Load** places the content, keeps it in the Content Conveyor, and then switches to the next item. This setting is useful if you want to cycle through all the items in the Content Conveyor without deleting them.

**Applying Load Conveyor**

You can also add items to the Content Conveyor using the Load Conveyor dialog box. This is more powerful than using just the Content Collector tool. Click the Load Conveyor icon in the Content Conveyor. This opens the Load Conveyor dialog box.

The Load Conveyor dialog box lets you enter the contents of multiple pages into the Content Conveyor.

Choose one of the following:
- **Selection** adds whatever content was selected on the page. This automatically creates a set if there is more than one item selected.
- **Pages** allows you to choose specific pages in the document. If you choose Pages, you can then use the drop-down menu to choose All Pages or one of the alternate layouts in the document. You can also enter specific page numbers in the Pages field.
- **All Pages Including Pasteboard Objects** adds the items from all the pages, including any items on the pasteboard. This is very helpful if you want to replicate all the items from one document in another.

Select the Create a Single Set check box to load all the items as a single group instead of as individual items.

# Linking Items

The Alternate Layout and Content tools allow you to create links between the original and copied items. This is very helpful if you make changes to the source item and want those changes applied to the duplicated items.

Linking text

When you create an alternate layout, select the **Link Stories** check box in the Create Alternate Layout dialog box (*shown on page 97*). This links the text from the source layout to the alternate layouts. The Create Link setting in the Content Conveyor sets a link between the text in collected and placed items.

TIP The relationship between the source item and the duplicate is sometimes called a parent/child relationship.

Updating linked text

When text is linked, the frame for the alternate layout text displays a link icon. When the source text has been modified, the link changes to a yellow alert triangle. Click the alert icon to update the alternate layout text to match the source text.

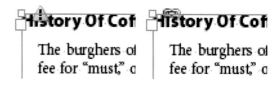

The yellow alert icon on the text frame on the left indicates that the source text has been modified. Click the alert icon to update the text. The link icon on the right appears.

You don't have to go scrolling through the document to find all the instances of the modified text. Open the Links panel. A yellow alert icon appears next to each text story. Double-click the alert icon next to each text story to update all the instances of that linked text. You can also hold the Opt/Alt key as you click one to update all of them at once.

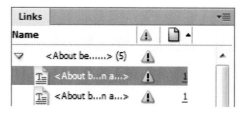

The yellow alert icons in the Links panel indicate the text that needs to be updated to match the source layout. Double-click the icon to update the text.

Releasing linked text

There may be times when you want the linked text to be different from the source. In that case it is best to free the alternate layout text from its linked state. Open the Links panel. The linked text is listed. Select the text and then choose Unlink from the Links panel menu. This removes the links between the text in the document. You can then modify the text in either layout without any alert icons.

TIP You need to be careful if you make modifications to the child text. If you then update the child text to match the parent text, those modifications will be lost. This is why we recommend modifying only the parent text, or unlinking the child text from the parent.

You can create linked content with both alternate layouts and the Content tools, but the Content tools give you additional features.

Select the **Create Link** check box in the Content Conveyor to link the child item to the original source. This creates two separate types of links — one for the item's content (text story or imported graphic) and another for the object itself (fill, stroke, size).

The Links panel with a linked story, linked images, and two modified linked objects.

Once you have links for objects, you can change the parent object's size, shape, appearance, or other attributes and then have those changes applied to the child objects. For instance, if you change the stroke color of the parent object, you can then update the stroke color of the child objects. Simply click the yellow alert icon to update the object listing in the Links panel.

You can modify which attributes of a linked item are part of the parent/child relationship by using the Links Info dialog box. Select the linked item (or items) and choose Link Options from the Links panel menu. Depending on which type of link you have chosen, either the Link Options: Story dialog box or the Link Options: Story and Objects dialog box appears.

The Link Options: Story dialog box controls stories that have been linked by using the Content tools or by creating an alternate layout. It allows you to set the following attributes:

- **Update Link When Saving Document** automatically updates a modified link when the Save command is applied to the document.
- **Warn if Link Update Will Overwrite Local Edits** shows an alert if the child story has been modified to be different from the parent story.
- **Remove Forced Line Breaks from Story** removes any forced line breaks when updating the parent and child text. This is useful when

the lines in the parent text have been forced to rag a certain way but the child text lines don't need those changes.

- **Define Custom Style Mapping** lets you choose how styles with one name in a document can be mapped to styles with a different name. (*For more information on this command, see the section "Mapping Styles" on page 112.*)

| Link Options: Story |
| --- |

☐ Update Link When Saving Document
☑ Warn if Link Update Will Overwrite Local Edits

Preserve Local Edits while Updating Object Links

☐ Appearance      ☐ Interactivity      ☐ Others
☐ Size and Shape  ☐ Frame Content

InDesign preserves edits made for the selected attributes.

☐ Remove Forced Line Breaks from Story
☑ Define Custom Style Mapping   [ Settings... ]

[ Cancel ]   [ OK ]

The Link Options: Story dialog box controls how linked stories are updated between the parent and child text.

If you have chosen the link for an object created using the Content tools, you have additional options in the Link Options: Story and Objects dialog box. This lets you to choose to **Preserve Local Edits while Updating Object Links**. The following attributes can be maintained even when the link is updated to match the parent content:

- **Appearance** maintains the fill, stroke, effects, and corner effects.
- **Size and Shape** maintains the transformation settings for size, shape, rotation, scaling, and skewing of an object.
- **Interactivity** maintains the attributes for buttons, forms, object states, animations, and timing.
- **Frame Content** maintains the settings for items within a group, for HTML code, and for Media panel settings applied to movies and sounds.
- **Other** maintains the settings for text wrap, hyperlinks, text frame options, and object export.

TIP The Size and Shape option is automatically selected if you drag with the Content Placer tool to create a custom size or shape for a linked object.

Preserve Local Edits while Updating Object Links

☐ Appearance     ☐ Interactivity     ☐ Others
☑ Size and Shape  ☐ Frame Content

InDesign preserves edits made for the selected attributes.

The Link Options: Story and Objects dialog box lets you preserve local edits applied to the child link when updating the object to match the parent setting.

# Linking Styles

You may find that the text styles applied to a story in one layout or page need to be adjusted for an alternate layout or page. There are two ways to control how text styles (paragraph, character, table, and cell styles) are applied to linked stories. The first is using *style groups*, which are created for alternate layouts; the second is using *style mapping*, which is applied to items linked using the Content tools.

Using style groups

As mentioned in the section on creating alternate layouts, you have the option to select **Copy Text Styles to New Style Group** in the Create Alternate Layout dialog box. This copies the text styles from the first layout into a new style group folder. These second styles are then applied to the alternate layout. Once you have these two style groups applied to the linked text, you can modify the style definition in one group without changing the appearance of the text in another group.

The new style group allows you to have different style definitions depending on the page size of the alternate layout. For instance, the point size for a print layout is often too small for tablet devices. Creating a new style group lets you modify the styles for the tablet device so the text is bigger. We have also seen situations where the horizontal layout for a digital magazine looks like the pages for a typical print magazine but the vertical layout has larger text without images. By creating new style groups, you can define the style for the horizontal layout with one point size and font while switching to a totally different size and font in the other. Even though the two layouts have different styles, their content is still linked.

Style groups for each layout as they appear in the Paragraph Styles panel. Notice that the styles have the same name but are contained in different style group folders.

| **History Of Coffee In Old New York** | **History Of Coffee In Old New York** |
|---|---|
| The burghers of New Amsterdam begin to substitute coffee for "must," or beer, at breakfast in 1668—William Penn makes his first purchase of coffee in the green bean from New York merchants in 1683—The King's Arms, the first coffee house—The historic Merchants, sometimes called the "Birth- | The burghers of New Amsterdam begin to substitute coffee for "must," or beer, at breakfast in 1668—William Penn makes his first purchase of coffee in the green bean from New York merchants in 1683—The King's Arms, the first coffee house—The historic Merchants, sometimes called the |

An example of what happens when different style groups are applied to alternate layouts. The vertical layout (left) has larger point sizes that work better for the longer column width. The horizontal layout (right) has smaller point sizes for the shorter column width.

Mapping styles

Mapping styles creates a similar result to style groups, but it gives you a little more flexibility.

When you use the Content Conveyor to duplicate items, you have the option to map the text style names from one story to different style names in the document or in other documents. This is especially helpful if you use the Content Placer to duplicate a text story in a separate document that already has a set of styles.

The style mapping controls in the Content Conveyor.

Choose **Map Styles** in the Content Conveyor. Then click the **Edit Map Styles** icon. This opens the **Custom Style Mapping** dialog box.

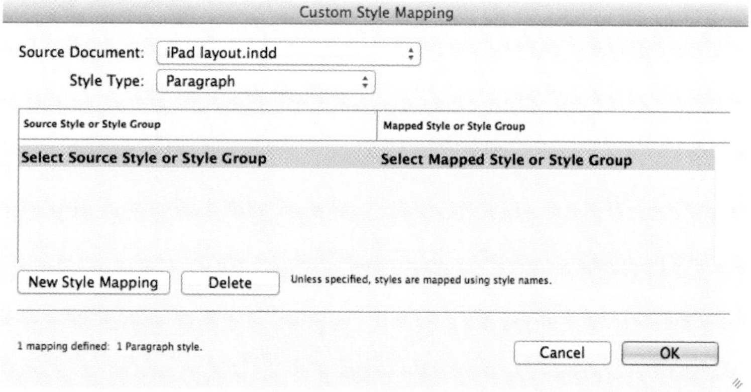

The Custom Style Mapping dialog box without any styles mapped.

---

TIP You can also open the Custom Style mapping dialog box by selecting a link in the list and choosing Link Options from the Links panel menu. Then select Define Custom Style Mapping and click the Settings button.

---

In the **Custom Style Mapping** dialog box, use the **Source Document** menu to choose the document that contains the styles you want to map. Choose a style from the **Style Type** menu; the options are Paragraph, Character, Table, and Cell.

Click the **New Style Mapping** button. The Select Source Style or Style Group controls appear. Click the Source Style or Style Group control (on the left) and choose a style from the list. Then click the Select Mapped Style or Style Group control and choose the alternate style that you want mapped to the source. Repeat these steps for additional styles that you want to map.

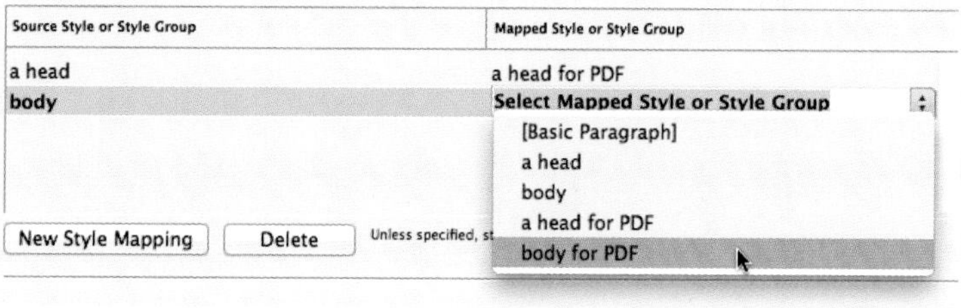

Choosing the mapped styles in the Custom Style Mapping dialog box.

---

TIP If you place items between documents, you need to switch to the second document in order to map to the styles found in that second document.

---

# Comparing Layouts

As you work with alternate layouts, you will probably want to compare how one layout looks next to another. The Split Window feature makes that easy to do.

Choose Window > Arrange > Split Window. This converts the document window into two parts. Each part displays a different alternate layout. Click a side to choose which alternate layout you are controlling. You can then use the Pages panel to choose different layouts for each side.

TIP Drag the name of a layout to move it in the Pages panel from one position to another. This makes it easier to compare layouts.

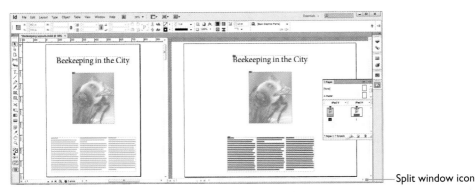
Split window icon

Using the Split Window feature to compare two layouts.

Choose Window > Arrange > Unsplit Window to restore the document to a single layout.

TIP You can also click the Split Window icons in the lower-right corner of the document window to split ⬛⬛ or unsplit ⬛ the layouts.

# Modifying Images and Text within Frames

With the exception of the Scale Liquid Layout rule, the text and images within frames are not affected by changes in size and orientation of pages. However, Liquid Layout rules do change the size of the frames that contain the images and text. InDesign has several features for adjusting the text and images within frames as the page size changes. For instance, what happens to the text and images when frames become wider? How does the text rewrap to fit the new column width? What happens to the image inside a frame? This is where you can use the **Auto-Fit** options for images, **Auto-Size** for text frames, and **Flexible Width** for columns.

TIP These features are not limited to working with Liquid Layout rules for creating alternate layouts; they can be useful when manually modifying frames.

Using the Auto-Fit options for images

Set the Auto-Fit options by choosing Object > Fitting > Frame Fitting Options. The Frame Fitting Options dialog box appears. When you select the Auto-Fit check box, the Fitting menu automatically changes to the default selection, Fill Frame Proportionally. This is the most useful setting for most images.

---

**Frame Fitting Options**

☑ Auto-Fit

Content Fitting
Fitting:  Fill Frame Proportionally  ⇕
Align From:  ▦

Crop Amount
Top: ⇕ 0 pt        Left: ⇕ 0 pt
Bottom: ⇕ 0 pt        Right: ⇕ 0 pt

☑ Preview                    Cancel        OK

---

The Frame Fitting Options dialog box lets you control how an image is treated when the frame resizes.

**Fill Frame Proportionally:** This resizes the image so that it completely fills the frame without any distortion. This is the best option if you want to make sure there is no empty space within the frame. No matter how much the proportions of the frame change, the image will always fill the frame completely.

Original image                    Frame resized

The Fill Frame Proportionally option applied to a frame. When the frame is resized, the image is scaled and cropped to fill the frame. There is no whitespace created.

---

TIP You can apply Frame Fitting options to an empty frame and the options will be honored when a graphic is placed in the frame.

---

Use the **Align From** reference box to set from what point the image fitting and cropping appears. Click the center point to keep the image centered in the frame.

Use the **Crop Amount** settings to specify the position of the image in relation to the frame. Positive numbers crop the image. Negative numbers add space between the image and the frame.

Select the **Auto-Fit** check box in order to have the image resize as the frame resizes. If Auto-Fit is not selected, the image only resizes when it is first placed into the frame.

Use the Fitting menu to choose how the image will automatically adjust. There are four options in this menu:

None: Applies no resizing to the image.

Fit Content To Frame: This resizes the image to fit in the frame. If the proportions of the frame change, this setting will distort the image. We almost never choose this option.

Fit Content Proportionally: This resizes the image to fit in the frame while maintaining the proportions of the image. If the image and the adjusted frame have different proportions, there may be some whitespace within the frame.

Fill Frame Proportionally: This is the default option as described on page 115.

Fill Frame Proportionally: This is the default option as described on page 115.

Applying the Auto-Size text controls

One of the worst things that can happen to your cherished text is that some of it disappears in an overset. The Auto-Size controls help you avoid that problem as text frames change size.

TIP The Auto-Size controls can also be used as you type directly into a text frame.

Select the text frame that you want to control. Choose Object > Text Frame Options to open the Text Frame Options dialog box.

Click the **Auto-Size** tab to display its settings. Choose one of the following from the **Auto-Sizing** menu:

- **Height Only** expands the top-to-bottom dimension of the frame.
- **Width Only** expands the left-to-right dimension of the frame.
- **Height and Width** expands both dimensions of the frame. This can change the frame's proportions.
- **Height and Width (Keep Proportions)** expands both dimensions but keeps the original proportions of the frame.
- **No Line Breaks** is available when you choose Width Only. It prevents the text from wrapping to a second line.

Use the Align reference box to set from what point the auto-sizing is applied. For instance, click the upper-left corner to have a frame that resizes its height and width down and to the right. Click the top middle point to have a frame that resizes its height downward.

The Auto-Size controls of the Text Frame Options dialog box.

You can also set **Minimum Height** or **Minimum Width** to maintain the minimum amount for either dimension. For instance, if the leading for your text is 12 points, a minimum height of 24 points ensures that at least two lines of text are always visible. This is very helpful to ensure that the frame doesn't collapse when the Liquid Layout adjustments are applied.

Setting Flexible Width columns

What happens when you change the orientation of a page from vertical to horizontal? Most likely, the width of the frame expands. This can make the column too wide to read comfortably. You need to make sure that the column width doesn't expand so much as the frame width increases. The best way to accomplish this is to increase the number of columns in the frame.

Instead of manually changing the number of columns when the page width expands, you can use the Flexible Width option for text frames. This option simply says that if the column width expands above a certain width, then another column will be created. This forces the column widths to be less than the maximum width. If the frame width continues to expand, additional columns are created as needed.

The Flexible Width option adds new columns as the width of a text frame increases.

The same thing happens as the width of the frame decreases. As the columns become thinner, one will be deleted if the remaining columns are below the maximum width.

To set Flexible Width columns, select the text frame and choose Object > Text Frame Options. With the **General** tab selected, choose **Flexible Width** from the Columns menu. Then enter a maximum width for the columns. When the text frame changes its width, the number of columns changes so that the maximum width is not exceeded.

The Text Frame Options dialog box set to the Flexible Width option for columns.

TIP You don't have to start with multiple columns to apply the Flexible Width option. A text frame with one column can still expand to multiple columns.

# Tablet Applications

# In This Chapter

WHEN STEVE JOBS INTRODUCED the iPad on January 27, 2010, the world expected another game-changing product from Apple. But few of us in publishing and design realized how profoundly it would change *our* world. Today, an increasing number of books and magazines are read with a swipe and a touch onscreen. Buttons and video are becoming as commonplace as editorials and classifieds. And the experience of reading is becoming much more immersive and engaging in the process.

InDesign is at the center of the publishing world for print, so it's not surprising that it has now become a key part of publishing to the iPad and other tablets. With InDesign and Adobe's complementary set of tools, known as the Digital Publishing Suite, a whole new world of design and interactivity has opened up to designers and publishers everywhere.

# Understanding Digital Publishing Suite Apps

Several third-party products allow you to convert your InDesign layouts to tablet apps for the iPad, Kindle Fire, or Android tablets. Most of them provide a set of free plugins for creating interactive overlay elements, along with some means of converting your documents into an app. Our focus in this chapter will be on Adobe's solution: the Digital Publishing Suite, also known as DPS.

Adobe's Digital Publishing Suite consists of several components that allow you to bring your InDesign layouts to life as applications on tablets that include the iPad, the Kindle Fire, Android tablets such as the Samsung Galaxy, and even the iPhone (though our focus throughout this chapter will be on tablet apps). The DPS tools allow you to add interactive features to your publication and to publish your file in a *folio* format that allows it to be shared and published to tablet devices.

DPS tools    DPS tools include several components. Each plays a different part in the process of creating a tablet app from your InDesign layout.

- **Folio Overlays panel:** An InDesign panel that allows you to add interactive features for tablets to your layout.
- **Folio Builder panel:** An InDesign panel that allows you to assemble your files into *folios,* which are files that can be previewed and shared.
- **Adobe Content Viewer (desktop version):** A computer application that allows you to preview your content and interactivity as it will appear on a tablet.

- **Adobe Content Viewer (device version):** A free application that is installed on your iPad (or other tablet) and allows you to preview your content and interactivity.
- **Folio Producer:** A browser-based application for organizing your folio files, adding metadata, and publishing folios.
- **Viewer Builder:** An Adobe AIR application that allows you to build a custom viewer app for your content that you can submit to Apple's App Store, Amazon's Appstore for Android, or Google Play.

The Folio Builder panel is part of the standard installation of InDesign CS6. When you first open the panel, you will be prompted to update the panel by clicking a link. This takes you to Adobe's website, where you can download the latest version of the DPS tools. Installing this package will add the Folio Overlays panel to InDesign and install the Desktop Viewer on your computer's hard drive. As the DPS tools are updated, the Folio Builder panel will prompt you to download the latest version.

To finally publish your app and make it available for sale requires that you sign up for one of three DPS subscription programs. At the highest and most expensive level are the Enterprise and Professional Editions, which are geared to mid-sized or large publishers. These allow publication of an unlimited number of single-issue folios or subscription-based, multi-issue folios (such as monthly magazines) on the iOS and Android platforms. Both also provide analytics, or data, about the folio downloads, with the Enterprise Edition offering additional services, such as the ability to create in-app custom navigation.

The Single Edition, which allows you to publish single-issue folios only, offers a more affordable entry point for small and individual publishers. In fact, the Single Edition will be made available to all Adobe Creative Cloud members for free. Non-subscribers to Creative Cloud have to pay a one-time license fee, which at the time of this writing is $395. The Single Edition is currently available for iPad only.

No matter which version you use, the tools and the creation process are the same. And anyone with an Adobe ID can use these tools to create and share folios with others.

One important thing to note is that the components of DPS are regularly updated, so you'll want to check out the resources mentioned at the end of this chapter.

DPS workflow overview     The basic DPS workflow involves multiple steps. The diagram below illustrates the overall process.

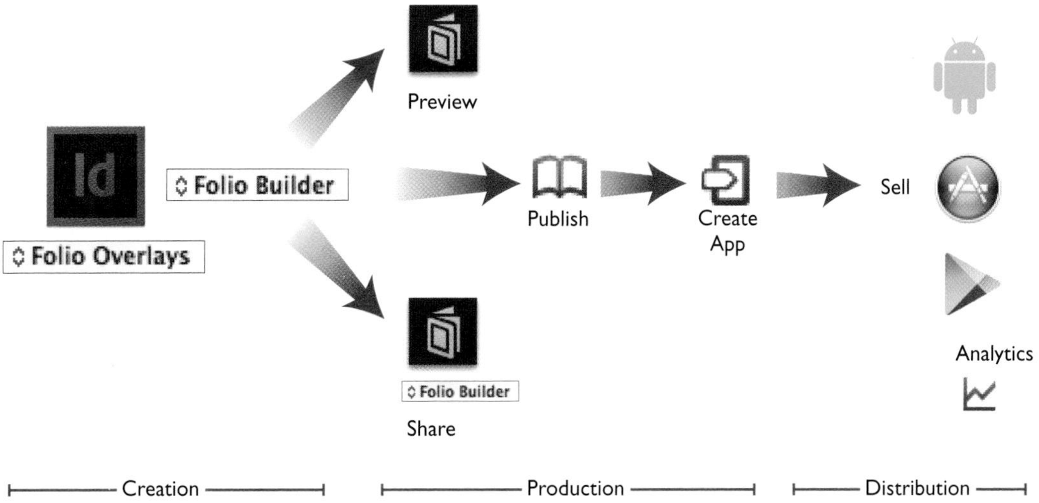

The basic DPS workflow includes adding interactivity to your layouts, using the Folio Builder panel to assemble them into a folio to preview and share, publishing the folio, and creating an app for sale in the appropriate marketplace.

The first step is to design your publication for viewing on a tablet and to add interactivity where appropriate. Design issues are discussed in the next section, "Design and Workflow Considerations" on page 125. Interactivity is added using InDesign's built-in features (*covered in Chapter 2*) and the Folio Overlays panel, discussed in the section "Interactivity and Digital Overlays," on page 130.

Next, your individual InDesign documents, called *articles*, are assembled into a folio, which you can think of as the file format for a tablet app. This assembly is done using the Folio Builder panel in InDesign, which is discussed in the section "The Folio Builder Panel" on page 157. You can also import HTML articles into your folio, but we're going to focus on working with InDesign files.

Once you've created your folio, you can preview it in a number of ways. You can view it on your computer by clicking the **Preview** button in the Folio Builder panel, which opens the Desktop Viewer. Or, install the Adobe Content Viewer on your iPad or other tablet, then sign in with your Adobe ID. The folio will then be available on your tablet. Both of these options are discussed further in "Previewing folios and articles" on page 167.

If you need to share your folio with others on your team or with a client, you can do so by clicking the name of the folio in the Folio Builder flyout menu and choosing **Share** from the menu. You can then enter multiple email addresses inviting others to view the folio. In order to view the folio, invitees must have an Adobe ID to sign in, and they can view the folio either on their tablet (using the Adobe Viewer) or in their Folio Builder panel in InDesign. See "Sharing folios" on page 170 for more information.

Once your folio is complete, use the Folio Producer to publish it to Adobe's distribution system, the first step to getting your app in the Apple App Store, Amazon's Appstore for Android, or Google Play.

**DPS app navigation and user interface**

Whether you create a folio to share with a few colleagues or publish your app for sale to the general public, all DPS apps allow you to navigate pages in the same way, and all share a common user interface, or *chrome* — controls that appear when the user taps the screen. The only exceptions are Enterprise Edition apps created with a custom interface. But the vast majority of DPS apps share the same "look and feel."

When you download the free Adobe Content Viewer for your tablet, you'll find an illustrated help file that explains this basic navigation and interface. It's also common when publishing an app to include a similar help file so that users unfamiliar with the interface can fully experience and engage with your app.

Most DPS apps are set so that you read an article by swiping vertically. The article may be set as individual pages or as one long, scrolling article. Swiping horizontally moves to the next article. However, a folio can also be set so that the user swipes horizontally only, much the way a print publication is read. With this navigation, the user basically swipes through every page of the publication.

When the user taps the screen, standard DPS navigation controls appear. These controls include the following icons:

- **Home:** tap to return to the app library.
- **Table of Contents:** tap to display the table of contents.
- **Previous View:** tap to go back to the previously viewed page.
- **Browse Mode:** tap to display thumbnail images of the articles.
- **Scrubber:** drag to scroll through the article thumbnails.

Home icon

Table of Contents icon

Previous View icon

Browse Mode icon

Scrubber

DPS apps have a standard interface for navigation, also known as the *chrome*. The user taps the screen once to display the chrome and can then navigate the app's pages.

# Design and Workflow Considerations

Although tablet apps are electronic, they still use the concept of "pages." But the design issues involved can be quite different from those encountered when designing for print. Interactive elements require a different way of thinking about how information is presented, and even about how the user is informed that elements of the page are interactive.

Another important difference is that many print publications, especially books and magazines, are really designed as facing-page spreads. Because the reader experiences both pages at once, they are effectively viewed as though they were a single page. When content moves to a tablet, there is no notion of spreads, and the overall design and design elements need to hold up in what are essentially single-page layouts.

**Page orientation: H, V, or both?**

One of the first decisions you need to make when converting a print publication to a tablet app is the orientation of the pages in the app. Because the iPad and most other tablets have a built in accelerometer, the screen rotates depending on how you hold the device. You can design your publication with pages that can be viewed in only a vertical orientation, only a horizontal orientation, or both vertical *and* horizontal orientations.

Some publications use only a single orientation. *Martha Stewart Living* (left) is vertical only, and *National Geographic* (second from left) is horizontal only. Others, like *Wired* (right and second from right), use both vertical and horizontal orientations.

There is no right or wrong decision regarding page orientation. One thing to keep in mind, though, is that creating a publication with both orientations is going to be more work than creating a single-orientation app. New features in CS6, such as Liquid Layout rules and alternate layouts (*discussed in Chapter 4*), help with the process, but building an app with both orientations still requires extra effort.

**Scrolling vs. individual pages**

Although tablet apps don't display pages in spreads like print publications do, the content still needs to hold up on its own page. One nice thing about pages on tablet apps is that they can be set as individual pages (similar to a print publication) or as scrolling pages (so that content is one continuous page that scrolls vertically).

The most common types of articles or pages that are set as scrolling pages are tables of contents, letters from the editor, credits, and colophons — "list type" articles. Other types of stories that are well suited to scrolling pages are articles that consist of short snippets of information, such as new product releases, new hot spots to visit, or anything that is essentially a list of items. On the other hand, long blocks of text such as feature stories can be harder to read in a scrolling view. It's usually best to set those types of articles in a page-by-page view.

Scrolling pages are easy to set up in InDesign. Simply make the InDesign page long enough to fit the article. For example, you might set a horizontal page to 1024 x 2000 pixels and a vertical page to 768 x 2000 pixels. (The maximum page size in InDesign is 15,562 pixels.) You can also set the article to Smooth Scrolling in the Article Properties dialog box, discussed later in this chapter.

Whether content is set up in individual pages or as one scrolling page, it's a good idea to give the reader some visual cue that more content is available. This cue could be a graphic image that you can see only part of, or it could be an arrow or other icon that points toward the rest of the article.

**Fonts and images**  Fonts look beautiful on tablets, especially on the Retina display iPad (2012), but that doesn't mean you don't have to make adjustments for tablet apps. When it comes to fonts, the main difference between layouts in print and on tablets is that very often body text that looks fine in print is too small on the tablet version. Most publications increase the body text size by at least 1 point or more, along with increasing any smaller text in the layout.

When you're working with images for tablet apps, there are a couple of things to keep in mind. Like fonts, images look fantastic on most tablets. But keep in mind that tablets use an RGB color space, so it's a good idea to keep your images in RGB whenever possible. You can download an ICC profile for the iPad at http://indesignsecrets.com/downloads/forcedl/ iPad.icc. Load this profile into all your Creative Suite applications, and you'll get more accurate color matching results.

You'll also want to keep your options open when cropping an image. Avoid destructive cropping. For example, you may crop an image one way for the cover of your vertically oriented print publication, but if you are creating a horizontal orientation for your tablet app, you'll need to crop the image differently, with more of the image showing on the sides.

Use high-resolution images for all non-interactive content. InDesign will automatically sample the images correctly for the device you're designing for. Some interactive content is sampled and some is not, as we'll discuss in later sections.

**Interactivity visual cues**  Part of what makes publications on tablets so compelling are the interactive features that can be included. There's nothing like buttons, slideshows, or movies to spice things up! Because interactivity is such an important part of the tablet app experience, it's important that your readers know it's there.

The most common way to guide users to interactive elements is to develop a series of icons that indicate different types of activity. These can be included on a help page at the beginning of your publication to let users know how to navigate and use the DPS controls that appear when the screen is tapped.

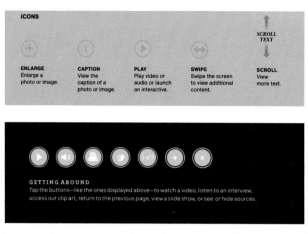

Indicate interactive elements in your app by developing a system of icons. These are the icons used in *National Geographic* (top) and *Martha Stewart Living* (bottom).

**Workflow considerations**

There are many issues regarding workflow when creating a tablet app publication, especially when it's in conjunction with a print version. We can't cover them all in detail here, but we'd like to mention a couple of very important things to consider.

First and foremost is the issue of resources. Whether you work on your own or are part of a workgroup, it takes time and energy to create a tablet app of your publication. Even with the tools that were added to CS6 to make the process of creating documents in multiple sizes and orientations easier, don't underestimate the additional work that's going to be involved. As we've been highlighting in this section, the design considerations for tablet apps are quite different from those for print.

Another part of the typical workflow that is affected is proofing. How do you proof interactive content? How do you mark it up for changes? Certain elements can be output from InDesign in PDF format, but many cannot, or not very easily. Imagine you have a slideshow created with object states, each of which includes an image and text. You could make a PDF, but you'd have to make one for each state, one by one, and this can be very time consuming.

---

**TIP** The most important step you can take in planning your workflow for creating a tablet app is this: Plan ahead!

---

If you know you will be creating both a print and a tablet app version of your publication, plan for both at the very beginning. Allocate resources, whether it's your own time or that of others, and right from the start, think about the assets as they relate to *both* your print version and your digital version.

# Setting Up Your Document

Part of the creation process for a tablet app is to set up your file properly. If you're creating a document, InDesign CS6 has a new intent in the New Document dialog box: Digital Publishing.

The Digital Publishing intent changes several default settings in the New Document dialog box, and it sets the Swatches panel to RGB when the document is created.

The Digital Publishing intent sets a primary text frame, which allows your text to reflow when you create alternate layouts. It also sets the Pages panel to display alternate layouts. Dimensions are set to pixels, pre-set page sizes for a number of popular mobile devices are listed, and the Swatches panel is set to RGB colors. Any of these settings can be changed, of course, and they can be captured for future use with the **Save Preset** option.

Keep in mind that many devices have an area that is used for navigation. For example, the iPad has a 6-pixel wide area on the right side of the screen that displays a scroll bar and crops the layout. You can download templates for the iPad that have guides to indicate parts of the screen that will be covered by the scroll bar or other parts of the interface at http://gilbertconsulting.com/resources-misc.html.

| Letter |
| A4 |
| iPhone |
| ✓ iPad |
| Kindle Fire/Nook |
| Android 10" |
| Custom... |

Pre-set page sizes in the New Document dialog box include several popular mobile devices.

# Interactivity and Digital Overlays

Many of the interactive features for tablet apps are added to your InDesign documents using the Folio Overlays panel. These elements are called overlays because when you create a folio, all the non-interactive elements in your layout are flattened to a JPEG, PNG, or PDF file, depending on the settings you use; the interactive elements sit on top of that, as an overlay.

Interactive elements are in an overlay that sits on top of the non-interactive elements in your layout.

One of the nice things about overlays is that they are maintained in both a horizontal and a vertical orientation, with no special action required on your part. As long as the same name is used for objects in each layout, the overlay will be consistent. For example, that means that if you are viewing the second slide in a slideshow in one orientation, the same slide is displayed when the user rotates the tablet.

Some of the interactivity that you can add to DPS apps is created using InDesign's native interactive features (*discussed in Chapter 2*), which can be used in PDFs as well as DPS apps. But most of these elements require some additional settings in the Folio Overlays panel, because of characteristics that are unique to tablets. For example, when you have a hyperlink to a website, you need to indicate whether the page will open directly within the tablet app or in the tablet's browser app.

Other interactive elements are unique to tablet apps, and these elements are added using the Folio Overlays panel. We'll discuss each of these in detail later in this section.

**Native interactive features supported**

Most, but not all, of InDesign's native interactive features are supported by DPS. The following table shows which native InDesign interactive features are supported and which are not.

| Feature | Supported by DPS | Not Supported by DPS |
|---|---|---|
| Animations | Not supported directly; animations must be converted to HTML5 and placed back in the InDesign file | |
| Hyperlinks | URL, email, Page, and Navto only | Text anchors and Shared Destination hyperlinks |
| Buttons | On Release event only; Go To First/Last page, Go To URL, Go To Page, Go To Previous/Next State, and Go To State actions only | On Click and On Rollover events; Go To Destination, Go To Next/Previous Page, and Show/Hide Button actions |
| Forms | | Not supported |
| Audio | MP3 files | |
| Video | MP4 files with h.264 encoding | |
| Bookmarks | | Not supported |
| Cross-References | | Not supported |
| Page Transitions | | Not supported |

The Folio Overlays panel extends the native features it supports by allowing you to add elements that are unique to tablet apps. But the panel also adds overlays that provide additional interactive features to DPS apps, including the following:

- Image sequencing
- Panoramas
- Web views
- Pan and zoom on images
- Scrollable frames

These features are created entirely using the Folio Overlays panel and, usually, a set of external files.

**Folio Overlays panel basics**

The Folio Overlays panel is essential to adding much of the interactivity to DPS apps. After you install the DPS tools from the Folio Builder panel, you can find the Folio Overlays panel under the Window menu.

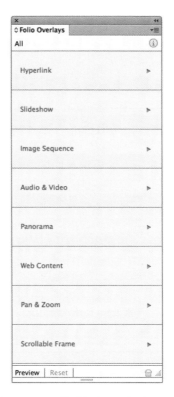

The Folio Overlays panel lets you access all of the interactive features you can modify or create for DPS apps.

Think of the Folio Overlays panel as your hub for adding interactivity to your DPS apps. It provides important tools for creating engaging experiences for your publication's readers, and previewing your work as you go along, either using the desktop Content Viewer or directly on your iPad.

**Creating links with buttons and hyperlinks**

Both buttons and hyperlinks play an important role in providing interactivity to DPS tablet apps. They provide navigation, allow us to play videos and sounds, click through slideshows, and link us to the outside world.

### When to use buttons vs. hyperlinks

Because both buttons and hyperlinks have similar linking functionality, it can sometimes be confusing to know when to use a button rather than a hyperlink. But they each have unique characteristics that when understood make it easy to choose the right feature for the job.

For one thing, only entire objects or frames can be made into a button; you can't select text within a frame and set a button, you can only set a hyperlink. That makes hyperlinks the only choice when you need to link selected text within a frame.

On the other hand, buttons are the only choice when you want the appearance of your link to change when it's tapped. Buttons have appearance options for Normal, Rollover, and Click, but only Normal and Click appearances are utilized by DPS. Only buttons let you jump to an object state, which is useful for slideshows, remote rollovers, or button "hot spots."

You can use either buttons or hyperlinks for similar kinds of links:

- To link to websites
- To link to other pages or articles
- To send email
- To link to other content

### Creating buttons for DPS apps

Creating a button for a DPS folio is the same as creating a button in InDesign for any other type of use, such as for a PDF file. However, there are certain events and actions that do not work in DPS apps and cannot be used. In fact, the only button event that is supported by DPS is **On Release or Tap**.

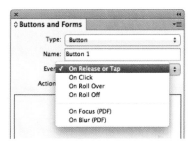

The only button event supported in DPS is On Release or Tap. The others have no effect when exported to a DPS folio.

There are also certain button actions that are not supported in DPS folios, including Go To Destination, Go To Next/Previous Page, and Show/Hide Buttons And Forms. None of the PDF Only actions are supported.

DPS supports the following button actions for hyperlinks:

- Go To First/Last Page
- Go To Page
- Go To URL
- Sound
- Video

DPS supports the following button actions for object states:

- Go To Next/Previous State
- Go To State

These actions are supported by DPS with no additional settings required. But whether you use buttons or hyperlinks, you must use the Folio Overlays panel to set how URL hyperlinks behave.

Use the Hyperlink settings to specify whether a link opens in the app (folio) or in a browser.

Panel settings

Open in Folio: By default, a website will open in the app, in an in-app browser, where all links on the website are fully functional. With this option, the user never leaves the app. To return to the app, the user simply taps the Done button in the upper-left corner of the screen.

Open in Device Browser: Choose this option if you want the user to be taken to the device's browser app, such as Safari on the iPad, when a link is tapped. With this option selected, the user will exit the app and go to the external browser. Always choose this option for email links, because you always want the user's email client to open to send a pre-addressed email.

TIP When setting a link to iTunes or the Apple App Store, use the Open in Device Browser option to avoid a Cannot Open Page error message.

Select the **Ask First** check box to specify that a prompt will appear, requesting permission to exit the app. It's usually a good idea to specify this prompt, so the user knows what's about to happen. Once the user is in the browser app, the DPS app has been completely exited and the app has to be re-opened.

Jump to another article

To create a hyperlink to jump to another article in your folio, use the **navto://** syntax. Then specify the name of the article as it appears in the Folio Builder panel, not as it appears in the Article Properties dialog box. (Both are discussed in detail later in this chapter.) Add a page number if you wish to link to a specific page in the article. When you're linking to a specific page in an article, keep in mind that the first page in the document is counted as page 0 (zero). So, for example, if you specify #3 in the URL, the link will jump to page 4. A typical URL to link to another article in your folio might be something like navto://*articlename*#3.

Creating slideshows with object states

Slideshows are just one of the many interactive elements that can be made using object states. In DPS apps, slideshows can be navigated by using buttons or by using tablet actions (such as Tap or Swipe) that are specified in the Slideshow section of the Folio Overlays panel.

As discussed in Chapter 2, you make an object state, also known as a multi-state object or MSO, by combining multiple objects into one. Select the objects — whether several images or a series of images grouped with text — and align them on top of each other using the alignment icons in the Control panel. Then in the Object States panel, click **New**, which groups the objects into a new object state.

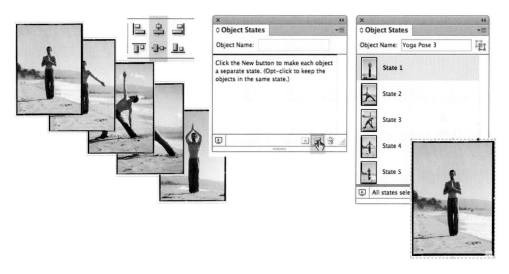

Creating an object state: Select a group of images and align them; click the Convert Selection to Multi-state Object icon in the Object States panel.

To allow the user to view the slideshow by tapping buttons that access a specific state or by browsing slide by slide, set the buttons to the Next/ Previous State action. Or, you can allow the user to view a slideshow without any buttons by selecting the appropriate settings in the Slideshow section of the Folio Overlays panel.

Panel settings

**Auto Play:** As soon as the user turns to the page, the slideshow will play; this is also known as "play on page load." If you select this setting, you can set a delay in the time it takes to play.

**Tap to Play/Pause:** The slideshow will play when the user taps the top image or state. If you select this option, it's a good idea to give some kind of visual cue, such as an icon or text, that clearly indicates that the slideshow should be tapped to see the action, since the user otherwise just sees the static image of the first slide.

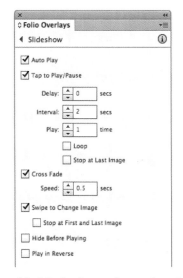

Use the Slideshow section of the Folio Overlays panel to specify settings for your slideshow.

Delay: If Auto Play is selected, you can specify a delay in the time between when the user turns the page and when the slideshow starts to play. You can specify from 0 (zero) seconds to 60 seconds. It's usually a good idea to set a small delay so the page elements have time to fully load before the slideshow starts to play.

Interval: If Auto Play or Tap to Play/Pause is selected, you can specify the amount of time each slide displays. The allowable range is 0.125 seconds to 60 seconds.

Play-Time: If Auto Play or Tap to Play/Pause is selected, you can specify how many times the slideshow plays. This option is not available when Loop is selected.

Loop: If Auto Play or Tap to Play/Pause is selected, selecting Loop will cause the slideshow to play continuously until the user double-taps the slideshow or turns the page. Many electronic document designers decry Loop as a distraction.

Stop at Last Image: If Auto Play or Tap to Play/Pause is selected, this setting will stop the slideshow at the last slide.

Cross Fade: This setting provides a transition fade to the next slide. The default time for the transition is .5 seconds, but you can specify any value from 0.125 seconds to 60 seconds. This applies to slideshows advanced manually or with Auto Play or Tap to Play/Pause selected.

Swipe to Change Image: This setting lets the user swipe from slide to slide.

Stop at First/Last Image: When Swipe to Change Image is selected, use this setting to specify that the slideshow stop on the first or last slide.

**Hide Before Playing:** If this setting is selected, the slideshow is hidden until it is triggered, either by user action or by other settings in the Folio Overlays panel.

**Play in Reverse:** Just like it sounds, selecting this option causes the slideshow to play backwards.

**Creating remote rollovers with object states**

Object states are used frequently in DPS apps because you can do so many different things with them. One common use of objects states is to create what is sometimes referred to as a "remote rollover."

Remote rollover usually refers to an effect where the user rolls over one part of a page onscreen and a change occurs in a remote (unconnected) part of the page. On tablets, there is no rollover state, so in this case it refers to when the user taps one part of the screen and a change occurs in another part of the screen. Remote rollovers can be created using an object state and buttons that go to specific states in the object state.

In this example, the user taps any one of four buttons to display a different yoga pose, along with how-to instructions.

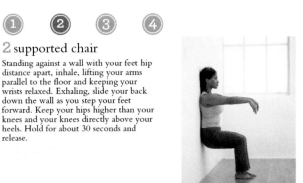

In this remote rollover, the user taps one of the numbered buttons to display a different yoga pose with instructions.

1.  The first step is to create each object state. A yoga pose image is positioned next to the text frame containing its instructions, and then the two are grouped.

2.  Once all four images are grouped with their instructions, the four groups are then aligned on top of each other and converted to an object state using the Object States panel.

3.  Next, the four buttons are created. Each button has a different image for the Normal and Click appearances. See Chapter 2 for information about using external graphics for button appearances.

4.  For each button, the event is set to On Release or Tap and the action is set to Go To *<the appropriate>* State.

1 tall warrior

With your feet three to four feet apart, point your right (front) foot forward and your left (back) foot slightly left. Keep your heels in line with each other and square your hips toward your right foot. Bring your arms overhead and inhale. As you exhale, bend your right leg until your knee is over your heel. Tighten the front of your left thigh. Hold for 4–10 breaths. Release. Repeat on the other side.

2 supported chair

Standing against a wall with your feet hip distance apart, inhale, lifting your arms parallel to the floor and keeping your wrists relaxed. Exhaling, slide your back down the wall as you step your feet forward. Keep your hips higher than your knees and your knees directly above your heels. Hold for about 30 seconds and release.

Each state is made up of an image grouped with instructional text in an adjacent text frame.

Each button is targeted to a specific state in the object state to create the remote rollover effect.

This technique offers a lot of flexibility, and with a little imagination and creativity you can produce a variety of engaging experiences for your users. You'll see this technique used in many of today's tablet publications.

Image sequencing

Image sequencing allows you to combine many images into a continuous series that can be stepped through by the user. It is particularly useful for creating a rotating 360° view of images or a time-lapse series of images.

Image sequencing is one of the interactive features that are unique to DPS, and it uses the Folio Overlays panel rather than the File > Place command to import the images used.

There are a variety of ways to create source images. One way is to use Adobe Photoshop Extended to export an image sequence of a video, whether a 3D object or a scene. Open the movie in Photoshop Extended, and use the File > Export command. Choose Render Video and change the settings in the dialog box as needed.

The Render Video dialog box in Photoshop. You can create the assets needed for an image sequence by opening a movie file in Photoshop Extended and exporting the frames as an image sequence.

You can also use Adobe Flash Professional or Adobe After Effects to export frames from an animation or a video. And, of course, you can use any 3D authoring application to generate images.

Images should be saved in JPEG format, or PNG if you wish to include transparency. InDesign won't compress the files in any way, so for JPEG files, use medium compression to keep your folio size down.

The files should be named with sequential ascending suffixes, such as image01.jpg, image02.jpg, image03.jpg, and so on. You also need to make the images the same pixel size as they will appear on the tablet; for example, 568 x 320 pixels.

TIP Use at least 30 to 60 images so their rotation will not be jerky. You usually don't need more than that, and using too many images will just make your file larger without a better result.

Combine all your images in a folder that will be just for these assets. You'll point to this folder to create the overlay.

monkey000.jpg  monkey020.jpg  monkey040.jpg

Image sequence files must be named with sequential ascending suffixes. Shown are three files from different points in a sequence.

The next step is to create a container frame in your InDesign layout and decide on the poster image you want to display. This will be the image the user sees when turning to the page. You can set the first image in the sequence as the poster, or you can use File > Place to insert an image that's not in the sequence as the poster.

If you want the first image in the sequence to be the poster, you can draw a frame of any size, because when you load the images the frame will automatically be re-sized to fit the content. If you want some other image to be the poster, place an image into a frame that is the exact size of the images in your sequence.

To import the images, select the container frame, and in the Image Sequence section of the Folio Overlays panel, click the **Load Images** folder icon at the top. Locate the folder containing the image assets.

Use the Image Sequence controls to load your images and to specify settings such as Auto Play and Swipe to Change Image.

Panel settings

**Show First Image Initially:** This setting will use the first image in the sequence as the poster and will re-size the selected frame to fit the image.

**Auto Play:** This will cause the image sequence to begin playing on page load.

**Tap to Play/Pause:** This setting will allow the user to tap the image sequence to begin playing; a second tap will pause it.

**Delay:** If you set the image sequence to Auto Play, this setting lets you set a delay before it starts playing. It's a good idea to set a short delay to give the page time to fully load before the image sequence starts to play.

**Speed:** This allows you to set the number of frames per second at which the sequence will play. It should not exceed the frame rate at which your images were sequenced.

**Play:** This setting lets you specify how many times you want the sequence to play.

**Loop:** This setting causes the sequence to loop, or play continuously, until stopped by a user action, such as a tap or a page turn.

**Stop at Last Image:** If Auto Play or Tap to Play/Pause is selected, this setting will stop the slideshow at the last slide.

**Swipe to Change Image:** This setting allows the user to swipe the image and move the images as slowly or quickly as desired, essentially allowing the user to step through the sequence.

**Stop at First and Last Image:** When Swipe to Change Image is selected, selecting this setting will stop the sequence at the first image and the last image. If this setting is deselected, the user can spin the image sequence continuously.

**Play in Reverse:** This setting will play the image sequence in reverse.

Working with audio overlays

You can include both audio and video files in DPS apps. Some of the properties for audio and video are set in the Media panel, as discussed in Chapter 2, and others are set in the Folio Overlays panel.

In order to include audio files in your DPS app, use the File > Place command to position an audio file in your InDesign layout. For DPS apps, the audio file must be in the MP3 format.

Next, you may optionally use the Media panel. You can use the Media panel to set the file to **Play on Page Load**, which automatically turns on the audio Auto Play option in the Audio & Video section of the Folio Overlays panel. You can also use the Media panel to set a simple poster for your video, but if you want a controller image for play and pause, for example, use the Folio Overlays panel, as discussed in the next section. Frankly, unless you want to set a single image for a poster, there is no particular reason to use the Media panel.

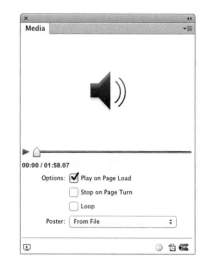

Some settings for audio can be controlled from the Media panel.

Next, you can set the audio file to play when the user turns to the page, or you can create buttons that the user can tap to play, pause, or stop the video. These options are discussed in more detail in Chapter 2. Alternatively, you can use controller files instead of buttons to allow the user to play or pause the sound file, as discussed in the next section.

Working with controller files

One of the interesting things you can do with the Folio Overlays panel is to set images to control the audio playback. You can create either a simple controller or a progressive controller, which shows the progress of the audio as it plays.

For a simple controller, you need only two files. However, they must have very specific names. Name the files with a _pause or _play suffix, such as audio_play.png and audio_pause.png. Add these two images to an assets folder that contains no other files.

Use the Folio Overlays panel to load a series of images that will display as a progressive controller bar, showing the progress of the audio as it plays.

Next, load the images by clicking the **Controller Files** folder icon in the Folio Overlays panel. Point to a folder that contains only the controller images. To use the *audio_play.png* image as the poster image, select the **Show First Image Initially** check box.

For a progressive controller, the images must be named in a very specific sequence that includes an increasing number, such as *audio01_play.png*, *audio01_pause.png*, followed by *audio02_play.png*, *audio02_pause.png*. As the audio plays, the images will be shown in a sequence that displays a visual of the audio progress. The total number of play files you use will be divided equally by the length of the audio. For example, if your audio is 30 seconds and you want the image bar to progress every second, create a total of 30 files, named *audio_play01.png* to *audio_play30.png*, with their corollary pause versions.

audio01_play.png   audio03_play.png   audio11_play.png   audio20_play.png

audio01_pause.png   audio03_pause.png   audio11_pause.png   audio20_pause.png

These images are part of a sequence that displays the progress of the audio as a controller that fills up from bottom to top as the audio plays.

It's also a good idea to create the images in the exact pixel size they'll appear in; scaling them up will cause pixelation, and scaling them down will make the file size larger than it needs to be. Use PNG or JPEG images with medium compression to best balance image quality and file size.

Because it can take quite a bit of time to create the images for a progressive controller (unless you automate the process; see the sidebar on the next page), it's a good idea to decide on a controller look that you want to use throughout your app publications. It can be very time consuming to change them all with each new issue.

## Using Illustrator to create audio controllers

Adobe Illustrator is the perfect application for creating the image sequence for an audio file controller. You can create objects for Start and Pause buttons and then use blends to precisely create the progress display. For example, if the audio takes five seconds to play, you create a blend with nine steps, including the start and end objects. This creates a player that runs for five seconds, with each step lasting half a second.

Once you've created the artwork, exporting PNG files from Illustrator is tedious. And if you need to make a small change, it's twice as tedious.

Adi Ravid has created for Illustrator a simple script, DPS Audio Player SkinMaker, that automates the process of creating those files and naming them correctly. You can download the script at *http://cookbooks.adobe.com/post_Audio_Player_SkinMaker_script-19701.html*. That page includes instructions for installing and using the script. Thanks, Adi!

Other panel settings

Auto Play: This setting is the same as **Play on Page Load** in the Media panel. It causes the sound to play when the user turns to that page.

Delay: If you set **Auto Play** in the Folio Overlays panel or **Play on Page Load** in the Media panel, only the Folio Overlays panel allows you to set a [**delay**] before the audio plays. It's usually a good idea to set a brief delay, even .125 seconds, so that the audio does not start playing before the page loads.

Use the Folio Overlays panel to set a delay on Auto Play, which helps prevent the audio file from playing before the page is fully loaded.

Working with video overlays

It's easy to include video files in DPS apps. As with audio files, choose the File > Place command to position a video file in your layout. For DPS apps, it's usually best to use a video file in MP4 format with H.264 encoding, which is compatible with Apple iTunes. Some of the settings for video will be set in the Media panel (*see Chapter 2*), and others will be set in the Folio Overlays panel.

It's most efficient to use a video that is the exact proportion and size in pixels as it will appear when played. For full-screen videos, make the width the number of pixels of the device you're targeting; for the iPad and iPad 2, for example, make the video 1024 pixels wide.

After you place the video, select it and open the Media panel. Select the **Play on Page Load** check box. This automatically turns on the video Auto Play option in the Audio & Video section of the Folio Overlays panel. You can also use the Media panel to set a poster for your video: None, Standard, a frame from the video, or an image file. The **Loop** option is not honored in DPS at this time.

Many of the settings for video files are controlled in the Media panel, which is used in conjunction with the Folio Overlays panel to specify the appearance of your video.

You can use the Media panel to set the appearance of the controller for the video, with controls for play, pause, and volume. You can also create buttons with actions assigned that play or pause the video, as described in Chapter 2.

The Folio Overlays panel options are a little different than those in the Media panel. Both panels are used to control how video behaves in your DPS app. The Folio Overlays panel includes three options for controlling video behavior.

Panel settings

Auto Play: While setting Play on Page Load in the Media panel sets Auto Play in the Folio Overlays panel, and vice versa, it's only in the Folio Overlays panel that you can set a **Delay** before the video plays. It's a good idea to set a brief delay, even .125 seconds, so that the video does not start playing before the page fully loads.

With these settings for video files, you can set a delay or specify whether the movie takes up the full screen when it plays.

**Play Full Screen:** This setting lets you specify that the video play in full-screen mode, whether via Auto Play or a tap on the screen. To return to the page after the video plays, the user taps the Done button in the upper-left corner of the screen.

**Tap to View Controller:** Setting this causes the controller to display when the user taps the video poster.

If you want to put an icon or other visual cue on top of the video file, simply place the icon on top of the video. When the user taps the video, the video, which is in a overlay, will move above the icon image and cover it while it is playing. When it is done, it will revert to the first frame of the video, with the icon image on top.

Place a visual prompt or icon on top of the video in InDesign (top). In the DPS app, the image will be visible on the video. When the user taps, the video plays in an overlay and the icon is hidden.

**Creating panoramas**  Panoramas let you put the user "inside" a locale and experience it as though the scene were viewed from a fixed location, looking around in all directions. For example, you could be inside a car and look around 360° or zoom in on the dashboard.

To create a panorama, you need six images that represent the six interior surfaces of a cube. If you have an existing panorama photo or image, convert it to six images. You can use Photoshop to stitch images together to create the initial panorama. Then you can convert the panorama to the required six images using a third-party utility such as Pano2VR, which is available in Apple's App Store.

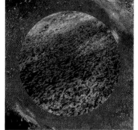

Images required to make a panorama. They show north, south, east, west, top, and bottom. Use the Folio Overlays panel to set exactly which parts of the images can be viewed.

Source files must be in JPEG or PNG format. Source files are not compressed by InDesign in any way, so to keep file sizes reasonable, use JPEG files with medium compression. The size of the panorama on the DPS page is determined by the first image, and the closer you can make the source images to their final sizes, the more efficient your final file size will be.

The six files must be named with ascending numbers, such as *pano1. jpg, pano2.jpg, pano3.jpg*, and so on. Copy all six images into their own folder, with no other files.

To import the images, click the **Load Images** folder icon in the Panorama section of the Folio Overlays panel and point to the folder containing the images. By default, the first image in the sequence will be used as the poster. Once this image is on the page, you can resize it as you would any graphic. However, as mentioned, it's best if the image is already sized.

Panorama images are imported using the Folio Overlays panel. The panel also includes settings for controlling what the user sees in the panorama.

### Panel settings

**Use First Image for Poster**: Selected by default. If you wish to use another image for the poster, choose File > Place to position it in the frame that will contain the six images.

**Initial Zoom**: This sets the initial zoom of the images when the user taps the panorama. Use a setting between the minimum zoom (30 percent) and the maximum zoom (80 percent).

**Vertical/Horizontal**: This lets you specify values that determine which area of the panorama is initially displayed. For Vertical, you can specify a value from −90 (tilted all the way up) to 90 (tilted all the way down). For Horizontal, specify a value from −180 (rotated all the way left) to 180 (rotated all the way right). The default of 0 (zero) sets the first image to display initially.

**Field of View**: This setting relates to how much the user can zoom in or zoom out, not to rotation.

**Limit Vertical Pan**: This setting limits the vertical tilt of the panorama. If you don't want users to be able to tilt through the image until it's upside down, set it to at least −1 and 1.

Limit Horizontal Pan: This limits how far the user can view the panorama to the left and the right.

**Web Content overlays** Web Content overlays allow users of your app to access all the resources of the web. Web Content overlays can be used for websites, RSS and Twitter feeds, or local HTML files.

To create an overlay to a website, first draw a frame of the dimensions and location of the desired view area. If you want to display a poster before the website displays, place an image in the view area frame; if you want the website to display when the page loads, leave the view area frame empty. The user's computer must have an Internet connection in order for the webpage to load.

InDesign layout with Folio Overlays panel settings

Tablet app page before and after user taps web area

To display a webpage from an external URL, type the URL in the Web Content section of the Folio Overlays panel.

Type the URL of the website into the panel. Remember, since your viewers will be using an iPad, you'll want to send them to the mobile version of the website (if there is one); for example, http://mobile.twitter.com/username.

If you want to display a local HTML page, draw an empty frame or a frame with a placed poster image for the viewing area. In the Web Content section of the Folio Overlays panel, click the **URL or File** folder icon and browse to the HTML file. The HTML file should be in its own folder, along with any resources, including images or scripts, that the HTML file refers to.

You can use this feature to display things like a Google map or Twitter widgets. Copy the code from the Google or Twitter page, save it in a file, and point to the file in the Folio Overlays panel.

A local HTML file should be in a folder with any assets or scripts the file refers to.

As shown in the table on page 131, InDesign animations are not currently supported in DPS. Animations in DPS can play only if they are converted to HTML5 files. You can start with InDesign's native animation features, discussed in Chapter 2, but then you must convert them HTML5 files.

One way to do this is to export your InDesign animations as Flash files (FLA format) and convert them using Adobe's experimental application Wallaby, available from Adobe Labs (http://labs.adobe.com/technologies/ wallaby/). Watch a video overview of this process on Adobe TV, at http:// adobe.ly/jWXPD8.

Alternatively, you can create the animations in Adobe's Edge software and save them to HTML5 in Edge's OAM file format.

Once the files have been converted to HTML5, the Web Content overlay option is used to display and play the animation.

Panel settings

Once you've set the URL or local file that the user will view in the view area frame, several settings can be adjusted in the Web Content overlay:

Auto Play: This setting will cause the webpage to load when the user turns to the page, without any tap necessary. You can also set a delay; it's a good idea to set a small delay so the page doesn't load before the rest of the app page appears.

Transparent Background: Select this option to set that the transparent background in a webpage be preserved. If this option is deselected, the web content background is used.

Allow User Interaction: This option lets the children play; that is, it lets the user interact with the displayed webpage, allowing them, for example, to click links and go to another page.

Scale Content to Fit: This option will cause the webpage to fit to the dimensions of the view area frame that you created. Be sure the frame is large enough that the webpage is still readable when it's inside the frame. If you do not select this option, the webpage will be displayed at actual size and will be cut off if the frame is not large enough to view the page, and in most cases users will need to scroll in both directions to view the page.

**Pan & Zoom overlays**

Pan & Zoom overlays allow your users to explore an image beyond what is displayed in the static view. Specifically, it makes a large image available in a small view area, allowing the user to tap the image and then pinch to zoom in or out, and move to parts of the image that are not seen in the static view.

To create an image for Pan & Zoom, make sure the image has the exact dimensions you want to use. For example, if you want users to be able to pan a 1024 x 1024 pixel image in a 300 x 300 pixel view area, create a PNG or JPEG image that is 1024 x 1024 pixels in 72 dpi. You can do this using Photoshop or Illustrator: Choose File > Save for Web & Devices, then specify the dimensions.

Draw a frame that will define the dimensions of the view area, and then place the image inside the frame. The image should be larger than the view area frame. Position the image so the view area contains the appropriate part of the image. Try to select a focal point or some part of the image that is interesting on its own. The image in the view area will essentially become the poster image.

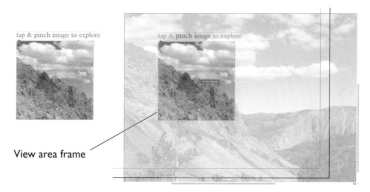

The view area (left) and the full image (right), which the user will be able to experience with Pan & Zoom enabled.

Once the image is positioned, select the image, including the view area frame. Use the Pan & Zoom section of the Folio Overlays panel to turn Pan & Zoom on.

The Pan & Zoom settings simply allow you to turn Pan & Zoom on or off for a selected image.

With Pan & Zoom, it's particularly important to let the user know that the images are not static images. Clear instructions or icons should be included on the page.

Once the user taps an image, the image can be scrolled or panned. The user can also pinch the image to see it reduced in the view area and visible in its entirety.

In this example, all three images are set to Pan & Zoom, and each image has been pinched and zoomed out to show the entire image.

**Scrollable frames**

Scrollable frames are unique to tablet apps. They allow the user to view more content on the same page by scrolling that content within a fixed area. Scrollable frames can contain text, images, other overlays, or any combination of content.

Scrollable frames are created using a container frame and a content frame. The content is positioned in the container frame using the Edit > Paste Into command.

For example, to create a scrollable text frame, place the text you wish to scroll in its own frame on the page. Draw another frame that is the size of the area you wish to be visible.

Container frame          Content frame

Scrollable frames require both a container frame, which will be the viewing area, and a content frame, which contains the content that will scroll.

Next, position the content frame so it displays the part of the text that you want to be visible when the page opens, and position it where you want it to appear in the container frame. Select the content frame, and use Edit > Cut to move it to the clipboard. Select the container frame, and use Edit > Paste Into to position the content frame inside the container frame. You can adjust the size of the container frame, which determines how much of the content frame will display before the text scrolls.

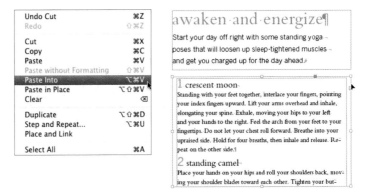

Cut the content frame, select the container frame, and use Edit > Paste Into to position the content inside the container frame.

Now you're ready to select the container frame, with the content inside, and use the Scrollable Frame section of the Folio Overlays panel to change settings for the behavior of the content.

The Scrollable Frame section of the Folio Overlays panel with default settings.

Panel settings

Scroll Direction: These settings determine the scrolling action of the enabled frames. **Auto Detect** determines the scroll direction based on the height and width of the container frame and content frame. For example, if the heights of the frames are the same but the widths are different, the content scrolls only horizontally. To make sure that the content scrolls in only one direction — even if the container frame is narrower and shorter than the content frame — choose **Horizontal** or **Vertical**. Choosing the **Horizontal & Vertical** option allows the content to scroll in both directions, assuming the content frame is larger than the container frame.

The direction options for scrollable frames.

Scroll Indicators: Select **Hide** if you don't want scroll bars displayed as the user scrolls the content.

Initial Content Position: Use this setting to determine the initial position of the content on the page. Select **Upper Left** to align the content frame to the upper-left corner of the container frame as the initial view. Select **Use Document Position** to use the location of the content frame as the initial view.

The "sliding drawer" effect

Because scrollable frames can have any kind of content, you can do all sorts of fun things with them. One of our favorite tricks is to make a sliding drawer, or pull tab, effect. This lets you make tabs that users can drag out to reveal additional content. The following steps show just one example of the kinds of things that can be created using this general technique. It has the advantage, too, of allowing you to include more content in the relatively small amount of screen real estate available on tablets.

1. Create and group the objects that will make up the tab content. In this example, we have the tab graphic, some text, and an image.

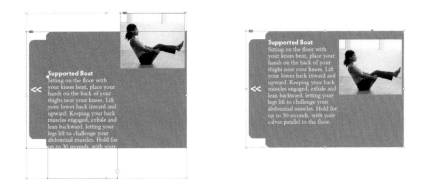

The content of the tab is created, in this case, with the gray tab graphic, some text, and an image (left). The objects are positioned and grouped (right).

2. Draw the container frame. Since our tab will pull out from the right side of the page, the height of the container frame should be the same as, or a little greater than, the content group. With a typical scrollable frame, at this point the content group would be cut and pasted into the container frame. But if we do that, the tab will not have a pullout effect. There just won't be that much room for the content to slide back and forth.

3. The trick to this technique is to draw an invisible rectangle that is positioned so that when it is grouped with the other content, the tab sits in just the right location in the container frame. This is illustrated on the following page.

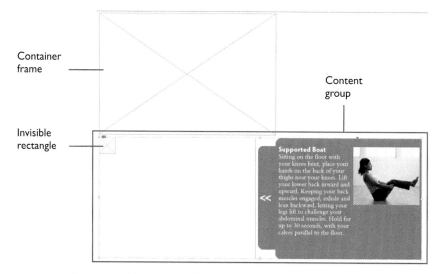

Container frame

Content group

Invisible rectangle

Supported Boat

Sitting on the floor with your knees bent, place your hands on the back of your thighs near your knees. Lift your lower back inward and upward. Keeping your back muscles engaged, exhale and lean backward, letting your legs lift to challenge your abdominal muscles. Hold for up to 30 seconds, with your calves parallel to the floor.

Draw an invisible rectangle and group it with the other content, which positions the gray tab in the correct closed position. You can adjust the position later if necessary.

4. Group the rectangle with the other content, then select Edit > Cut to move it to the clipboard. Select the container frame and choose Edit > Paste Into to create the scrollable frame. You can click the content group and position it as needed once it's pasted into the container frame. If the invisible rectangle is not in the correct position, double-click it to select it within the group and move it to the appropriate location.

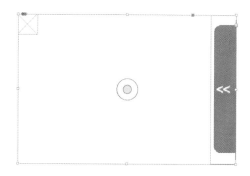

Use Edit > Paste Into to position the content group in the container frame. If the tab location needs to be adjusted, double-click the rectangle to select it within the group and reposition it.

5. In the Folio Overlays panel, choose Horizontal from the Scroll Direction menu. And finally, select the **Hide** check box so that a scroll bar doesn't appear when the user slides the tab out.

The result, as viewed in the Desktop Viewer, is a pull tab, or drawer, that the user taps and pulls out to reveal the content. The tab can be moved back and forth at will by the user.

# The Folio Builder Panel

The Folio Builder panel in InDesign is an essential part of creating a DPS app. The purpose of the Folio Builder panel is to assemble your documents into a folio file that can be converted into an app. The panel allows you to set properties for the folio; preview your work, including the interactive components; and share your folios with others for review.

*Exploring the Folio Builder panel*

The Folio Builder panel is used to create a folio file that will ultimately become a standalone app, such as a book or a single issue in a multi-issue app (as in a monthly magazine). Folios are made up of articles, which in turn are made up of layouts. Each folio may contain multiple articles. Each article may contain a layout that is horizontal only, vertical only, or one of each, depending on how the folio is set up.

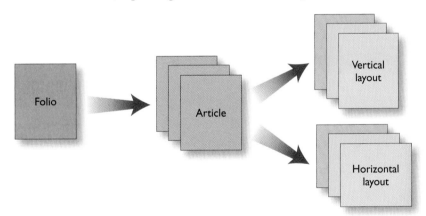

A folio consists of articles, which are made up of InDesign layout files.

The Folio Builder panel is a multi-level panel. It displays folios when you are working on folios, articles when you are working on articles, and layouts when you are working on layouts. The key to using the panel is to pay attention to the label at the top of the panel, which tells you which level is being displayed.

The key to using the multi-level Folio Builder panel is to keep an eye on the top of the panel, which shows you if you are viewing folios (left), articles (center), or layouts (right).

To navigate to the next level, click the arrow to the right of the folio or article, or double-click the folio or article name. To go back up from a layout or article, click the left-facing arrow at top.

When you are viewing folios and articles, the bottom of the panel will have a **Preview** button, a **New** or **Add** button, and a **Trash Can** icon to delete folios or articles. When viewing layouts, you can Add a layout only if you are missing either the horizontal or vertical version.

The buttons at the bottom of the Folio Builder panel let you preview the entire folio (left), an article (center), or an individual layout (right).

When you have a list of multiple folios, you can filter which ones are displayed. At the top of the panel, click the black triangle next to **Folios: All**. You'll see a list of the various kinds of folios that can be listed. The default setting is **In the Cloud** (that is, uploaded to the Acrobat.com web host), but there are other options that are discussed later in this chapter. Regardless of how you filter the list, you can also sort the list of folios alphabetically, by most recently modified, or by publication date.

You can filter the kinds of folios that are displayed in the Folio Builder panel, and sort the filtered list.

Creating a folio

The first step to creating a folio is to open the Folio Builder panel (Window > Folio Builder) and log in with your Adobe ID. If you already have an Adobe ID you wish to use, choose **Sign In** from the panel's flyout menu; choose **Sign Up** if you don't have an Adobe ID or want to create a new one.

## DPS and your Adobe ID

If you've ever registered your Adobe software, you have an Adobe ID. It's free and is your usual "identifier" to Adobe. Most people have just one Adobe ID.

However, be aware that the Adobe ID you use in the Folio Builder panel will be tied to a specific custom viewer app that is created later in the process. This means that if you have different publications, you'll want to sign in using different Adobe IDs. The folio you create may be a standalone app, such as a book, or it may be a single issue in a multi-issue app, such as a monthly magazine. Either way, the steps to create a folio are the same, but only one Adobe ID can be associated with a publication's viewer app.

Next, click the **New** button at the bottom of the Folio Builder panel to display the New Folio dialog box. Here you will set various important attributes of the folio, including the **Name** of the folio. The name of the folio will be used for production purposes, and is not the name users will see in the final app.

You can also specify the **Viewer Version**. The viewer version is associated with the version of any viewer app you've previously built, or the Adobe Content Viewer on your device used to preview your work. To change the version for the folio, click on the version number in the New Folio dialog box; the Viewer Version dialog box will display, then select the appropriate choice. You'll want to make sure that your folio is an equal version or lower than any viewer app you'll want the folio viewed in.

TIP To determine the version of the Adobe Content Viewer on your tablet device, go to any app in the Library. Tap once to display the navigation controls, then tap twice on the name of the publication at the top of the screen. The version and build number will display.

Specify the **Size** of the folio, which should be the same aspect ratio as your articles. The folio doesn't need to be exactly the same size, but the same aspect ratio is important; for example, 4:3 for iPads or 16:9 for Android tablets. You can also set the **Orientation** of your folio to contain only horizontal, only vertical, or both horizontal and vertical articles.

By default, when you create a folio it is uploaded to the Acrobat.com web host. However, if you don't need to share the folio or preview it on another workstation, you can select the **Create Local Folio** check box. This will save the folio to your local hard drive, a good alternative when you want to work quickly or don't have an Internet connection. Local folios are indicated by a disk icon 🖴 next to them.

The New Folio dialog box lets you define several important settings for your folio, including size, orientation, and image format.

Image format options let you specify the format of the flattened part of the folio. Remember that your InDesign layout is flattened to an image, with the interactive elements in an overlay. The options are JPEG, PNG, and PDF.

**JPEG** creates an efficient file size and is ideal for most tablets. You can also set the **Default JPEG Quality**, or compression, to Minimum, Low, Medium, High, or Maximum; the default is High, which gives good results on most devices. This setting can be changed when adding new articles to the folio. **PNG** format is required, however, for transparency effects.

**PDF** folios are often the best choice, because they hold their resolution regardless of the device resolution. PDF folios work best for the Retina display on the third-generation iPad, but they can also be used for the iPad 1 and 2. However, at this time PDF folios do not preview in the Desktop Viewer, which means they must be uploaded to the cloud in order to be previewed. This is cumbersome and takes time for each preview.

Adding a single article

Once you've created a folio, you can add the currently active InDesign document to the folio as an article. Click the folio name to go to the Articles level, then click the **New** button at the bottom of the panel. This displays the New Article dialog box.

New Article

Article Name:

Cover

Default Format:

Automatic ▼

JPEG Quality:

High ▼

Portrait Layout:

iPad_v ▼

Landscape Layout:

iPad_h ▼

Smooth Scrolling:

Off (Snap to Page) ▼

Cancel        OK

The New Article dialog box lets you name an article, and if you have used alternate layouts for the two orientations, it will load them automatically.

In this dialog box, specify a **Name** for the article. This does not have to match the document file name and should relate to the content of the article in some way. This name is also used for creating links between articles, but it is not displayed to the end user in the viewer app. For instance, an article called "How to Train Your Cat" might be named "Cat" in the Folio Builder panel.

You can also specify the **Default Format** of the non-overlay components of the article: JPEG, PNG, or PDF.

If your InDesign document uses alternate layouts and contains both horizontal- and vertical-orientation pages, these will be automatically loaded for the **Portrait Layout** and the **Landscape Layout**. If the InDesign document is set up as a long scrolling page, you can turn on **Smooth Scrolling** for the page; the default is Off (Snap to Page).

If your InDesign file contains only one orientation, open that file or make it the currently active document file, and then create a new article. When you click OK, the file is added to the article and the orientation of the document is determined automatically. Once that file is loaded, make the file with the other orientation the active document. Then double-click the name of the article in the Folio Builder panel and click the Add button. The file will be added and the orientation automatically determined.

If you have only one orientation layout in each InDesign file, make one orientation active and create a new article, then make the other orientation file active and click the Add button.

## Importing articles

Instead of adding articles one by one, you can import a folder of several articles at once. The file names and organization on your hard drive must be very specific, however. Start with a folio folder that contains article folders. When you import, you'll point to the folio folder.

The folders for articles with both horizontal and vertical orientation must contain two InDesign files. One must have an _h suffix and one must have a _v suffix, such as *filename_h* and *filename_v*. If the article has a single orientation, the InDesign file within the article folder must have the correct orientation suffix.

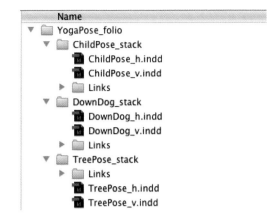

The file structure and naming conventions must be very specific in order to import articles.

To import articles, first create a folio in the Folio Builder panel. Next, choose the **Import** command from the flyout menu on the panel. You can import one or more articles.

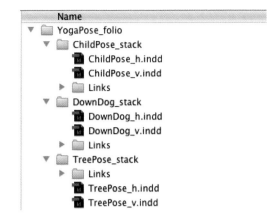

To import multiple articles into a folio, choose the Import command and target the folio folder containing the article folders.

Once InDesign has imported the article folders, the articles are listed in the Folio Builder panel. You'll still need to modify the article properties, as discussed in the next section.

The imported folders are added as articles and will appear in the articles list for the folio.

Setting folio and article properties

After you create a folio, you can set the properties for the folios and articles. These properties specify what will appear in the app and be seen by the user, unlike the production-related settings you assign when first creating the folio.

Setting folio properties

To access the Folio Properties dialog box, click the name of the folio in the Folio Builder panel. From the flyout menu, choose **Properties**.

Folio properties are set after the folio is created and can be accessed from the flyout menu in the Folio Builder panel.

Use the Folio Properties dialog box to set the **Publication Name** of the folio; this is the name that the user will see in the viewer app and is different from the folio name in the Folio Builder panel. You can also change the **Viewer Version** number, which specifies the version of the viewer app your folio will be viewed in. Be sure the version number of the folio is equal to or lower than the version of the viewer app.

Use the Folio Properties dialog box to set the name and to preview the icons that will appear in the viewer app.

The folio is represented in the viewer app library by a preview image. These images should be 72 dpi JPEG or PNG files and the same pixel dimensions as your folio, such as 1024 x 768. To load the preview, click the **Folder** icon and point to the image file. If you want to change the image, select it, click the **Trash Can** icon to delete the image, and load a new one.

Setting article properties

As with folio properties, the information and images in the Article Properties dialog box will be seen by the user in the viewer app. Article properties you can add include information like that often seen in print publications, such as the title and the author's name (byline), along with additional information about the content.

To access the Article Properties dialog box, click the name of an article in the Folio Builder panel. Next, choose **Properties** from the flyout menu.

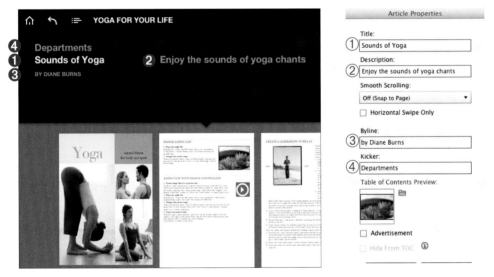

The Article Properties dialog box is displayed by clicking an article and choosing Properties from the flyout menu.

The **Title** of the article is displayed when in Browse mode in the viewer app and also in the table of contents. The title here is different from the name of the article used in the Folio Builder panel; the article name in the Folio Builder panel is used for creating links between articles but is not displayed to the end user in the viewer app.

The Article Properties dialog box lets you specify the title, description, byline, and kicker that will display for each article in the viewer app.

The **Description** of the article will appear above the article in the viewer app. This text could be similar to what's called a *deck* in magazine articles — text that usually sits between the title and the body text — and further explains what the article is about.

If you're working with an article that you want to scroll as one long page, change **Smooth Scrolling** to the direction you want it to scroll. If you have an article made of individual pages, you can set them to **Horizontal Scroll**, which causes the pages to no longer display vertically within an article, but horizontally only, so the user goes through the article page by page.

The **Byline** will appear below the title in the viewer app. The byline is usually where the author's name would appear.

The **Kicker** will appear above the title in the viewer app. It will also display above the title in the table of contents. This is often used to designate the different sections in a publication, such as Departments or Features. But this is not a hard and fast rule, and you can use it for any text that makes sense in this context.

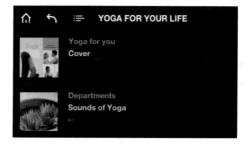

The Kicker and Title text display in the table of contents in the viewer app, along with the thumbnail preview specified in the Article Properties dialog box.

To specify an image for the table of contents thumbnail, click the folder icon next to **Table of Contents Preview.** Select an image that is 70 x 70 pixels and 72 dpi, in JPEG or PNG format. If you don't specify an image in the Article Properties dialog box, a table of contents icon is automatically generated from the first page of the article.

If your folio contains a page that is an advertisement that you don't want to appear in the table of contents, select the **Advertisement** check box. If it's some other kind of article you don't want to appear in the table of contents, select the **Hide From TOC** check box.

**Previewing folios and articles**

It's important, of course, to be able to preview your folios, articles, and interactive layouts. But even single pages, if they contain interactive settings or elements created using the Folio Overlays panel, will not preview in the SWF Preview panel. Instead, use the Folio Builder panel to access the Adobe Content Viewer.

There are two versions of the Adobe Content Viewer: a desktop application and a mobile device application. The Desktop Viewer is automatically added to your computer when you install the Folio Producer tools. The viewer for mobile devices is available for download in the Apple App Store, Google Play, and Amazon's Appstore for Android.

Preview on your computer

The desktop version of the Adobe Content Viewer provides a quick and easy way to preview folios, articles, or even individual pages in your layout, right on your computer screen.

It does have some limitations, though. You cannot preview an entire folio at once if it contains both dual-orientation articles and single-orientation articles. But you can still preview individual articles within the folio. Another limitation is that you cannot preview PDF folios, at least at the time of this writing.

To preview a folio, select it in the Folio Builder panel. At the bottom of the panel, click **Preview** to display the menu. Choose **Preview on Desktop** to display in the Desktop Viewer on your computer.

The Desktop Viewer displays the folio and all its articles. There are several shortcuts you can use to mimic viewing the folio on a mobile device. Use Cmd/Ctrl with the + and – keys to simulate pinching in and out.

| View | |
| --- | --- |
| ✓ Portrait | |
| Landscape | ⌘R |
| Zoom In | ⌘ + |
| Zoom Out | ⌘ − |
| Fit in Screen | ⌘0 |
| Actual Size | ⌘1 |

The Desktop Viewer uses keyboard shortcuts to allow you to view a folio as you would on a mobile device.

---

**TIP** Use Cmd/Ctrl-R to rotate orientation in the Desktop Viewer.

---

To view an article in the Desktop Viewer, select the article in the Folio Builder panel and click the **Preview** button at the bottom of the panel.

If you're working with 1024 x 768 pixel documents, you can also preview your current open InDesign file. Choose File > Folio Preview, and the Desktop Viewer will preview the file. This will preview the file even if it hasn't been added to a folio and can come in handy when you don't have an Internet connection and can't get to your folio in the cloud.

| File | |
| --- | --- |
| New | ▶ |
| Open... | ⌘O |
| Browse in Bridge... | ⌥⌘O |
| Open Recent | ▶ |
| Folio Preview | |
| Folio Preview Settings... | |

Folio Preview lets you preview your current layout file in the Desktop Viewer.

You can control the image format of the Desktop Viewer by choosing File > Folio Preview Settings and selecting the image format in which to display previews. Select **Preview Current Layout** if you want the Desktop Viewer to display only your current layout.

You can also preview the interactive content on your current page using the Folio Overlays panel. Click the interactive content on the page to access the appropriate section of the panel, then click **Preview** at the bottom of the panel.

The desktop version of the Adobe Content Viewer is a good "quick and dirty" way to preview your work, but it doesn't precisely emulate the experience your users will have when viewing your app. You should always check your work periodically by previewing it on the target device.

### Preview on your device

You can also preview folios and articles on an iPad, an iPhone, or Android tablets. That way, you'll know exactly how your app will look and feel on its destination device.

There are two different ways you can preview folios. In both cases, you must have the Adobe Content Viewer installed on the target device. Download the app from the appropriate store for your device.

You can preview your folios from the cloud (that is, on Acrobat.com). Simply go to the Adobe Content Viewer on your device and log in with the same Adobe ID you used to create your folios. Once you sign in, all your folios in the cloud will be available for downloading and previewing. Local folios will not be available for preview.

You can also preview your folios and articles without an Internet connection by connecting your iPad, iPhone, or Android tablet to your computer. To view your folio and articles, the device must be physically attached to your computer, and the Adobe Content Viewer must be open. To preview a folio, select it in the Folio Builder panel. At the bottom of the panel, click **Preview** to display the menu. Choose **Preview on** <*device name*>. The folio will appear in the Library window of the Content Viewer.

You can preview folios and articles by connecting your device to your computer, without any Internet connection required.

There are a couple of advantages to previewing on your device with a direct connection. For one, you can often preview folios and articles more quickly, as no Internet connection is involved and you don't have to wait for your articles to upload and then download. Also, you can preview local folios with a direct connection.

Keep in mind that the Adobe Content Viewer is basically a generic version of an app viewer, and its primary purpose is for testing your digital content directly on the iPad, iPhone, or Android device. The Adobe Content Viewer is updated along with the Folio Producer tools, which are updated frequently.

**Sharing folios**

While the ultimate goal of your tablet app is its publication to a wide audience, it's also important to be able to share your interactive content with others who are part of a smaller group, especially during the development process. Fortunately, the Folio Builder panel makes it easy to share folios and articles with other members of your workgroup or with your client.

To share a folio, select it in the Folio Builder panel and choose **Share** from the flyout menu. The dialog box that is displayed lets you send an email to the person, or group of people, with whom you'd like to share the folio. You can input multiple email addresses separated by commas. The default subject line reads "*<your name>* has shared a folio with you." Fill out the Message field to include a message with the email. Click the **Share** button, and an email will be sent to the addressee(s).

| Share |
|---|
| Share folio with:      ⓘ |
| johndoe@johndoe.org |
| Subject: |
| DIANE BURNS has shared a folio with you |
| Message: |
| John, |
| Let me know what you think. |
| Thanks |
| Cancel    Share |

The Share option in the flyout menu of the Folio Builder panel lets you send an email to members of your workgroup or to your client, allowing them to preview the folio.

Once you've shared a folio, the folio name will be displayed with a share icon 🏠. Hover your cursor over the folio name to display a tool tip that includes information about the folio, its owner, and how many people have shared it.

A tool tip displays information about the folio, such as that it has been shared with one person.

The person with whom you've shared the folio must log in using their Adobe ID in order to view the shared folio. In fact, you must send the email to the email address used by their ID in order for them to be able to view the shared folio. The folio will be available in the Folio Builder panel on their copy of InDesign, as well as in the library of the Adobe Content Viewer on their iPad or Android tablet.

If you want to stop sharing a folio, choose **Unshare** from the flyout menu on the Folio Builder panel. A dialog box displays a list of all the users sharing the folio. You can unshare with any individual member of the list or unshare the folio from the entire list.

If someone shares a folio with you, that folio will display in your Folio Builder panel and in the library of your device's Adobe Content Viewer. You'll see the folio in your Folio Builder panel list with the share icon next to it, but when you go to the articles list, the article names will be grayed out (meaning you cannot change them, but you can preview them).

**TIP** You cannot share local folios from the Folio Builder panel. Instead, move them to the cloud. From the flyout menu on the Folio Builder panel, choose Upload to Folio Producer, which puts the folio in the cloud so it can be shared.

Sharing folios is the method used by advertisers to submit ads to publications. The advertiser shares the ad folio with the publication. The ad can then be added to the publication's folio in Folio Producer, the next step in the publishing process.

# Folio Producer

After you've created your interactive content and added your folios with articles to the Folio Builder panel, the next step toward creating an app is to upload your content to Folio Producer. Folio Producer is a web-based tool that allows you to organize, edit, share, and publish the folios you've created in InDesign. It's part of the DPS Dashboard, which contains several tools and resources for publishing your app.

Because the focus of this book is on the tools in InDesign, we'll just give you a quick overview of Folio Producer to get you started exploring on your own.

To access Folio Producer, choose **Folio Producer** from the flyout menu on the Folio Builder panel or use your computer's browser to log in to the DPS Dashboard at http://digitalpublishing.acrobat.com. Log in with the same Adobe ID you used to create your folios in the Folio Builder panel in InDesign. Anyone with a valid Adobe ID can log in to the DPS Dashboard, but certain options are available only to DPS subscribers.

Sign in to the DPS dashboard using the same Adobe ID you used to create your folios in the Folio Builder panel in InDesign.

From the Dashboard, click **Folio Producer**. You will now be in the **Folio Producer Organizer** and will see a list of all the folios you created in the Folio Builder panel in InDesign. From this list view, you can specify various settings for the folio, such as the **Publication Name** and the **Folio Number**. Settings that are marked with an asterisk are required to publish the folio. Any changes you make here are updated and show in your Folio Builder panel in InDesign.

You can also share the folio from here by clicking the Share icon [image] at the top of the window. Just as when sharing from the Folio Builder panel, you'll get an email you can address to invite others to share the folio.

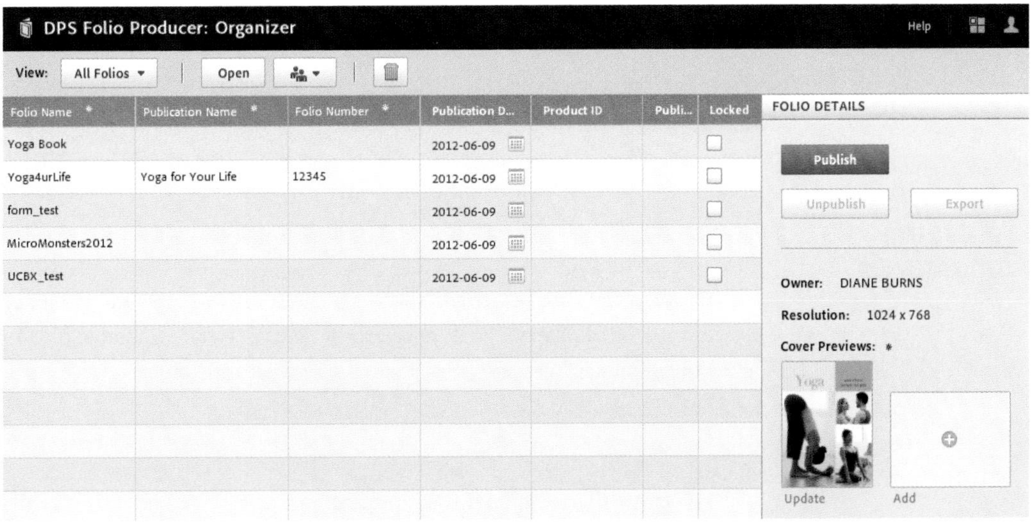

The Folio Producer Organizer lists all the folios from your Folio Builder panel in InDesign. Changes made here are reflected in the folios in the Folio Builder panel.

If you have local folios you want to work with in Folio Producer, you must upload them. Click the name of the local folio and choose **Upload to Folio Producer** from the flyout menu. The list in Folio Producer will be updated to include the local folio.

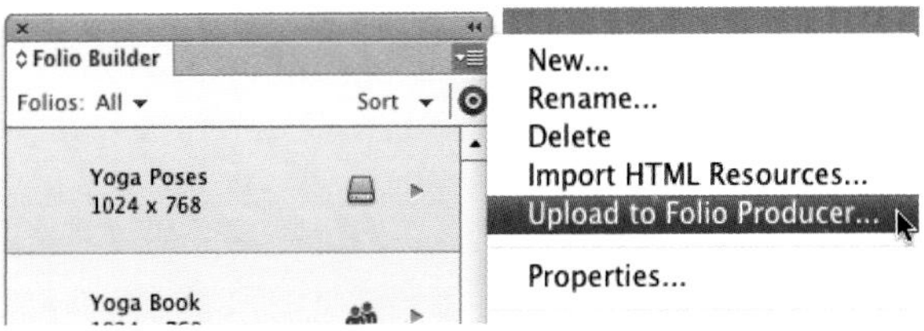

To list local folios, upload them to Folio Producer from the Folio Builder panel in InDesign.

You can use the **Folio Producer Editor** to rearrange articles, move articles to and from other folios, and change article settings. To access the Editor, click the name of a folio in the Organizer list and click **Open**.

You can work with articles in either a thumbnail view or a list view. To change the article properties, click an article and edit the information shown on the right side of the window.

The Folio Producer Editor lets you rearrange articles or change article properties.

You can still edit your InDesign documents after you have done work on them in Folio Producer. From InDesign, choose **Update** from the flyout menu on the Folio Builder panel.

Once your folio is organized the way you want it, you can publish your folio to the Adobe Distribution Server. This option is available to anyone and does not require a DPS subscription. Simply click the name of the folio in the Folio Producer Organizer window, then click **Publish**. Once the folio is published, you can download it to your device's Adobe Content Viewer and experience the app exactly as your users will see it.

If you have a DPS subscription, you will need to embed this published folio in your custom viewer app. The folio is embedded in the viewer app as a ZIP file. To create this ZIP file, click the **Export** button in the Folio Producer Organizer window.

The final step in Folio Producer is to export your folio as a ZIP file that can be embedded in the app.

Think of the Folio Producer as a bridge between the production of your folio and the actual app development, which requires a DPS subscription. The app development is the final step in making your app available for sale to the general public.

# What's Next: Publishing Your App to a Store

The final step to selling your app to the public is to turn it into an actual device application. As we mentioned in the first chapter of this book, designers and creative professionals are expected not only to be creative and produce documents, but also to become application developers. Details of the process are beyond the scope of this book, but we offer an outline of what's involved to get you started.

Once you've published your folio and exported it, the next step is to build a viewer app. The Viewer Builder app can be downloaded from the DPS Dashboard, where you signed in for Folio Producer. Use the Viewer Builder wizard to name your app, add icons and splash screens, and point to the ZIP file of the folio created using Folio Producer.

If you are publishing to the iPad or iPhone, you'll need to sign up to become an Apple Developer. The cost is $99 a year, and you can sign up at https://developer.apple.com/programs/ios/.

Amazon has its own requirements for developers for the Kindle Fire, details of which can be found at http://developer.amazon.com/. There is yet another set of guidelines for Android developers, which can be found at http://developer.android.com/index.html.

# Resources

As mentioned at the beginning of this chapter, the details of creating apps using the Digital Publishing Suite are quickly changing. The features of the Folio Builder panel and Folio Producer, the details of DPS subscriptions, and the final process of development will all change frequently.

Here is a list of important resources that will supplement this book and bring you the most up-to-date information about DPS.

- Robert Bringhurst, author of the documentation for InDesign and the Digital Publishing Suite, has created a fantastic publication app for the iPad called *DPS Tips*. It's a must-have app if you want to learn more about DPS: http://itunes.apple.com/us/app/digital-publishing-suite-tips/id436199090?mt=8
- The Adobe Help files for DPS are available online: http://help.adobe.com/en_US/digitalpubsuite/home/

- The DPS Developer Center has fantastic resources, including white papers and videos: http://www.adobe.com/devnet/digitalpublishingsuite.html
- There are many excellent videos covering DPS on Adobe TV: http://tv.adobe.com/product/digital-publishing-suite/
- Adobe provides a gallery of all the publications that have created DPS apps — a great source of inspiration, and a list that is growing daily: http://blogs.adobe.com/digitalpublishinggallery/
- Don't forget to check out our blog. We'll add information as it becomes available on new features and processes for creating tablet apps using DPS: http://www.indesigndigitalpublishing.com/

# ePubs and HTML

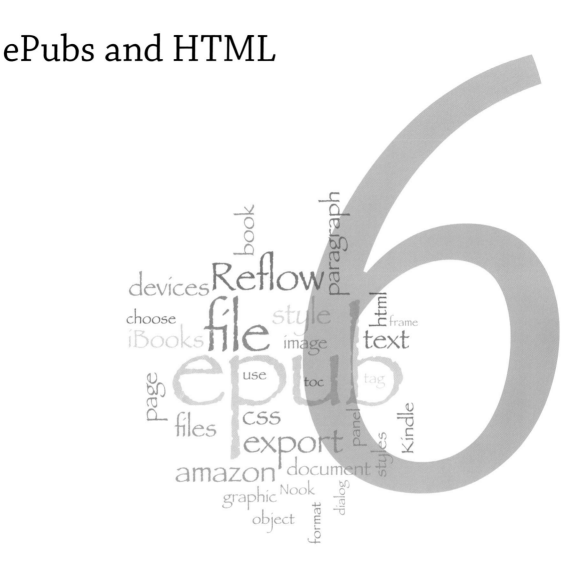

# In This Chapter

ONE OF THE MOST PROFOUND CHANGES in our digital world has been the rapid rise in the acceptance and embrace of eBooks by the general reading public. Those stacks and shelves of beloved volumes, with their dog-eared pages, have been replaced by a single, sleek eReader that can contain hundreds of books and takes up almost no shelf space at all.

You can see the change anywhere you go — on airplanes and subways, in waiting rooms, and even at the beach. You're as likely to see a Kindle or Nook as you are a paperback or hardcover book. And as the weeks and months go by, eBooks make up an increasing percentage of publishers' sales. (Are you reading this book on paper or a screen?)

Many of us remain nostalgic about paper books, and they are not likely to completely disappear any time soon. But the convenience and environmental benefits of eBooks ensure that they, too, are here to stay.

It turns out that another aspect of our digital world—viewing information on websites coded with HTML—has a lot in common with ePub, the standard format for eBooks. Under the hood of every ePub is actually HTML and CSS code. In fact, many of the options for exporting InDesign files to ePub are the same as those for HTML. There are, of course, some significant differences, including the way in which the files are ultimately viewed, but understanding one format will help you understand the other.

# Understanding ePub

An eBook is an electronic book — any book that can be read on a desktop or laptop computer, a tablet device, or a smartphone. Technically, when we talk about an *eBook*, we're referring to all kinds of electronic books in different formats, which could include PDF or HTML files. But *ePub* is a *format* for eBooks, and in this chapter we'll specifically explore the features of the ePub format.

The ePub file format is an open eBook standard developed by the International Digital Publishing Forum (IDPF). It was established in 2007 and replaced the Open eBook standard.

An ePub file can be read on a variety of hardware ePub readers, like the Amazon Kindle, the Barnes & Noble Nook, and the Sony Reader. It can also be read by software running on many platforms: the iBooks application on an iPad or iPhone; Adobe Digital Editions, Nook, or Kindle readers on OS X or Windows; Aldiko Book Reader on Android devices; and dozens more.

What distinguishes ePub files is that they are designed for reflowable content, whereas a print layout is considered a fixed layout. The way an ePub will be viewed on different devices varies greatly, because it adjusts to the screen size available. Furthermore, most ePub readers allow the user to adjust the font family and size of the text (*see the illustration on page 181*).

Reflowable content can display only one stream of text and anchored graphics, so it can be a mind-blower seeing your carefully laid out fixed-layout page seemingly fall apart the first time you export an ePub file from InDesign!

Because an ePub file is so different from the fixed format you create in InDesign, it requires a steeper learning curve than does a file format like interactive PDF, where the layout is maintained. You'll need to learn what information you'll lose when you export an ePub file, along with how to prepare your file in InDesign before exporting.

You may also be surprised to know that many of InDesign's interactive features cannot currently be used in ePubs. That will change over time, but for now it's important to know the limitations.

| InDesign Feature | Supported by ePub | Not Supported by ePub |
| --- | --- | --- |
| Animations | | Not supported |
| Hyperlinks | Yes, all types | |
| Buttons | | Not supported |
| Forms | | Not supported |
| Audio | Yes, MP3 files | |
| Video | Yes, MP4 files with h.264 encoding | |
| Bookmarks | | Not supported |
| Cross-References | Yes | |
| Page Transitions | | Not supported |

*Like creating a mini website*  When you create an ePub file, it's helpful to visualize the process as being similar to creating a mini website (*see "Going Under the Hood," later in this chapter, on page 204*). In fact, the settings in the EPUB Export Options dialog box are very similar to those in the HTML Export Options dialog box. That's because an ePub file is a compressed package (a ZIP file) that consists of HTML or XHTML files, CSS (Cascading Style Sheets), and some XML files. As on a website, the HTML indicates the structure, such as identifying a top-level heading. The CSS formats the heading to a particular size and weight and indicates how much spacing will appear on all sides of it. We'll give you an introduction to the structure of an ePub file, and a few basics about working with CSS, later in the chapter.

When InDesign creates an ePub file, it performs a conversion. It exports the objects in your document (text and graphics primarily) in a particular order. It translates the formatting that you have applied to text and graphics into a CSS style sheet. Other information you have added to the document, like a table of contents and *metadata* (information about the book), is exported as well.

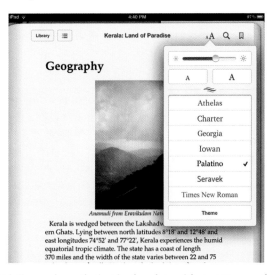

Readers of ePub files can change the font family and size of the text. These are the settings in the iBooks application on an iPad.

**Losing information when exporting**

Because you're converting from a fixed layout to a reflowable one and translating InDesign styles into CSS styles, you'll lose much of the InDesign document's formatting in the process. Much of it can be retained by carefully preparing your InDesign file before ePub export.

Only the text and graphics on your document pages are exported. Any objects on your master pages, including headers, footers, and page numbers, are skipped during the export. (Since the pages of an ePub file will flow very differently on a laptop than on a smartphone, your fixed-layout page numbers won't be useful.)

In a print book, you might start each part of your front matter (title page, acknowledgments page, and so on) on a separate page. Because page breaks in your fixed layout will be discarded, they must be re-created in a different way when exporting an ePub.

The exact positions of unanchored images or sidebars will be lost. To be retained, they need to be anchored in the text.

And some kinds of InDesign formatting are lost altogether. Any InDesign-created objects (lines, frames with no content, and so on) will be ignored. Paragraph rules are discarded.

## Can I read an ePub on my Kindle?

Sadly, the popular Kindle eBook readers don't support reading ePub files directly. They use a much simpler, HTML-based format called *MOBI* or *Kindle*.

At the end of this chapter, we'll tell you some ways to turn an ePub file created in InDesign into this format. It sometimes requires special preparation of the InDesign file, or it may require some tweaks to the CSS template that InDesign creates.

*ePub workflow*  Creating an ePub requires following a workflow to capture the maximum amount of information from the InDesign document. This requires you to format your text with styles. You also need to establish the export order of the text and anchor any graphics or sidebar text. You may need to make adjustments to graphics formatting and add information such as a table of contents or metadata.

After making the correct settings in the EPUB Export Options dialog box, you'll view your ePub file in an ePub reader. For example, you can download and use the free Adobe Digital Editions ePub reader.

It's a good idea at this point to do an initial *validation* of the ePub, which means running a version of EpubCheck. This ensures that it meets the requirements of the ePub specification required for your eBook to be published. We'll tell you about this at the end of the chapter.

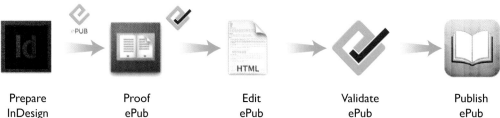

| Prepare InDesign File | Proof ePub | Edit ePub | Validate ePub | Publish ePub |

Creating an ePub file from InDesign requires following a series of steps. These include preparing your InDesign file and proofing, editing, and validating the ePub before publication.

Often, you'll discover that corrections need to be made in the InDesign file. For example, you may discover that some of your images aren't named correctly, whch will cause validation to fail. Images need to be named as they would be in a website, so exclude spaces and certain special characters.

Other changes or corrections may need to be made in an HTML editor. Some formatting, for example, may not come through correctly when viewed in an ePub reader. Not all readers will display your ePub in the same way. It's much like the early days of web development, where every browser created its own display. Other formatting—for example, paragraph rules—has to be added to the CSS style.

The last step is the final validation of your file. Once it passes, you'll be ready to publish your ePub, either through a bookstore or on your own website.

## Preparing Files: Creating Reading Order

As we described, you can't just use the ePub export function in InDesign and expect that it will instantly produce a perfect ePub. You have to set the order of export, style your text carefully, work with your images, and add some additional information to your document.

InDesign uses its own export order, which is rarely what you want! It looks at the objects in the document, starting with those closest to the left edge and beginning at the top, and then it exports objects farther down at the same vertical position. It then moves to the right, adding other objects from top to bottom.

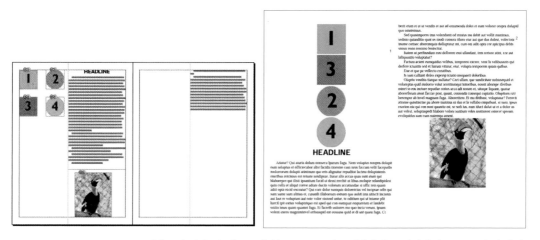

When the InDesign layout (left) was exported to ePub, InDesign's default export order kicked in, top to bottom and left to right. The results are shown in the Adobe Digital Editions ePub reader (right).

A story is considered a single object, and all text in the story is exported before going to the next object—even if this means going all the way to the last page of the document and then back to an earlier page. There can be only one text flow, so any sidebar objects or graphics that aren't anchored would be dumped at the bottom.

Layout order

The most basic way to create a proper reading order when exporting to ePub is to use layout order. If you are building a very simple document, like a novel, you can simply create the objects (such as text frames) in the document in the order in which you want them exported.

This is the only method to use when the text in your document flows as a long story in one thread. The key is to anchor images and other blocks of text in the main story flow so they will appear in the anchored location. Anchoring objects is simple: Simply drag the blue icon on the object's frame to the location at which you want it to appear in the text. You may want to create an extra paragraph return so the object is anchored on its own line, depending on how you want the final object to be positioned.

In the EPUB Export Options tab of the General panel, choose **Based on Page Layout** from the Content Order menu. The document will be exported with the images and other anchored objects positioned in the main text flow.

XML structure

A second method uses InDesign's somewhat obscure XML structure panel. Select the **Same as XML Structure** option in the Content Order menu. Creating XML is beyond the scope of this book, but Cari Jansen describes this method in a blog post: http://carijansen.com/2010/09/18/moving-print-publications-to-epub/.

Articles panel

For complex documents with many elements, an easier and more intuitive method for ordering the content is to use InDesign's Articles panel (Window > Articles).

The empty Articles panel will give you instructions for what to do. Drag your first object onto the Articles panel, and you'll be prompted to name your article.

TIP You can name the article anything you like, because it is not exported to the ePub file.

To set the export order, reposition the objects in the Articles panel in the order in which you want them to appear. This overrides InDesign's left-to-right, top-to-bottom order. You don't have to move any objects around on your pages to set the order. When you export, choose **Same as Articles Panel** in the Content Order menu.

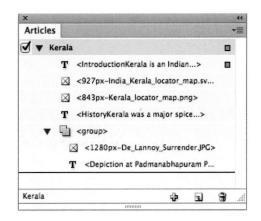

Drag one or more objects onto the Articles panel to begin establishing the export order for the article.

You can create a new article by clicking the New Article button at the bottom of the panel. Having multiple articles makes it easier to move large groups of objects up or down the list. Any article that has **Include When Exporting** selected will be exported to the ePub file in the order in which it is listed on the panel.

TIP You can also hold down Cmd/Ctrl and click the + button at the bottom of the panel to add all objects in the document to the current article.

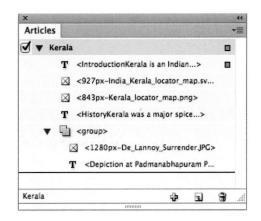

Once you have added text frames, graphics, images, and groups to an article, you can drag them up and down to rearrange them. You can delete an object by selecting it and clicking the Delete All Items (trash can) button.

# Preparing Files: Using Styles

Another important process in preparing your document for ePub export is consistently applying styles. While styles are always important in formatting text and objects consistently and quickly in InDesign, it turns out they are essential for ePub export! Creating and applying styles is a basic skill that we don't cover in this book, but if you need to learn how to work with styles, we recommend Sandee's *InDesign CS6 Visual QuickStart Guide*.

Paragraph and character styles

When you export a document as an ePub file, InDesign's paragraph and character styles are converted into CSS. The relative size and weight of a heading will be retained, as well as the space around it (indent, space after), but other information is discarded. For example, if you have a Heading1 style that is defined as Minion Pro Bold 18/19 with 12 points of space before and 5 points of space after, all that information — except space before — is converted into the CSS. However, if you also have a paragraph rule defined to appear below the headline, that information will be discarded. (Space before may be included in a future InDesign update.)

```
39 ▽h1.heading1 {
40      color:#000000;
41      font-family:"Minion Pro", serif;
42      font-size:1.5em;
43      font-style:normal;
44      font-variant:normal;
45      font-weight:bold;
46      line-height:1.056;
47      margin-bottom:5px;
48      margin-left:0px;
49      margin-right:0px;
50      text-align:left;
51      text-decoration:none;
52      text-indent:0px;
53 }
```

When InDesign converts the Heading1 style definition into CSS that is applied to `h1` elements with the class `heading1`, the font family, size, leading, and color become CSS properties. Space after is converted into a margin setting, but the paragraph rule in the InDesign style is not included.

If you have used local overrides instead of styles, select the Preserve Local Overrides option on the Advanced panel of the EPUB Export Options dialog box, and InDesign will attempt to write CSS attributes to reflect the relative sizes, weights, and spacing. It will even try to retain the spacing provided by multiple paragraph returns. However, this will create very messy and difficult-to-edit CSS code and is not recommended. Using paragraph and character styles consistently is definitely the way to go.

TIP If you're converting an InDesign-created ePub file to Kindle format, be aware that the Kindle may discard the formatting of paragraphs with local formatting. Using styles in this case is critical.

**Object styles**     When you are including frames containing graphics or sidebars in an exported ePub, InDesign designates each of them with an HTML <div> tag. A <div> tag simply divides the HTML code into a section that controls more than one attribute for the elements and applies CSS styles to many elements at once. InDesign will attempt to include the frame formatting (background color; border weight, color, and style; and the spacing inside and outside the frame) into the CSS for the particular <div> tag.

However, InDesign gives each <div> a generic name, which makes it difficult to identify them. By applying an object style with a descriptive name, you can better identify it in the HTML code.

For example, you can define the Sidebar object style with a background color, a stroke width, and a stroke type and color and then apply it to the sidebar frame. When you look at the HMTL code in an HTML editor, you can more easily identify the <div> because it contains the style name. The CSS reflects the size of the frame as well as the border style and width, the fill color, the padding (inset on text frame), and the margin (on text wrap).

```
<div class="Sidebar frame-14">
    <h3 class="sidebar-head">Climate</h3>
    <p class="Sidebar-Copy">With 120-140 rainy days per year, Kerala has a wet and
        maritime tropical climate influenced by the seasonal heavy rains of the
        southwest summer monsoon. In eastern Kerala, a drier tropical wet and dry
        climate prevails. Kerala's rainfall averages 122 inches annually. Some of
        Kerala's drier lowland regions average only 49 inches; the mountains of eastern
        Idukki district receive more than 197 inches of orographic precipitation, the
        highest in the state.</p>
    <p class="Sidebar-Copy"> </p>
</div>
```

Creating and applying a Sidebar object style makes it easier to identify the HTML <div> code after the file is exported.

**Table and cell styles**     Table and cell styles applied to a table are converted into HTML table tags and CSS. Border color, border style, border width, and background color are retained. It's important to use table and cell styles, because if you just apply table formatting locally, it will not carry over to the CSS.

**Mapping styles to tags**     By default, InDesign maps all paragraph styles to HTML <p> (paragraph) tags. But HTML is designed to give semantic meaning to content. It's a good idea to leave the <p> tags for body copy, but you should map headers to HTML header tags —<h1>, <h2>, and so on.

## How much code do you need to know?

How much does a print designer need to know about CSS and HTML to be successful with ePubs? Whether you are a freelancer doing all your own work or working for a large company that has a several different players, you should *at the very minimum* know how to set paragraph styles, character styles, and object styles in InDesign.

If you're working on a simple book with a single story and no special graphics, you can simply apply paragraph and character styles and map them to tags.

But if you're going to work on anything more than the simplest of documents, you really should understand how those styles come through in CSS format, and you should at least be familar with what CSS looks like. Beyond that, you may either edit the CSS yourself or have a more experienced person do it for you. It is not trivial to become fluent in coding, but some designers and creative professionals choose to do so because they're interested in it or because their job requires it. See the section "Going Under the Hood" on page 204.

You can map styles in the Export Tagging pane of the Paragraph Style Options dialog box. Choose the paragraph style you'd like to tag (for example, Heading1), and choose Style Options from the Paragraph Style Options panel menu. In the Export Tagging pane, select between `<p>` and heading tags; for example, for a Heading1 (first-level head), apply an `<h1>` tag.

It's also helpful to apply the name of the paragraph style (with hyphens instead of spaces) to the `class` name. A class helps pinpoint which elements the CSS is being applied to. A tag can be associated with several different classes, each applied to different elements.

Similarly, character styles can be mapped to tags in the Character Style Options dialog box. For italic, you would usually apply an `<em>` (emphasis) tag; for bold, you would apply the `<strong>` tag. Although entering a class name of *italic* or *bold* is not required, it creates clearer CSS. These are applied as classes in an HTML `<span>` tag to a range of words inside another tag.

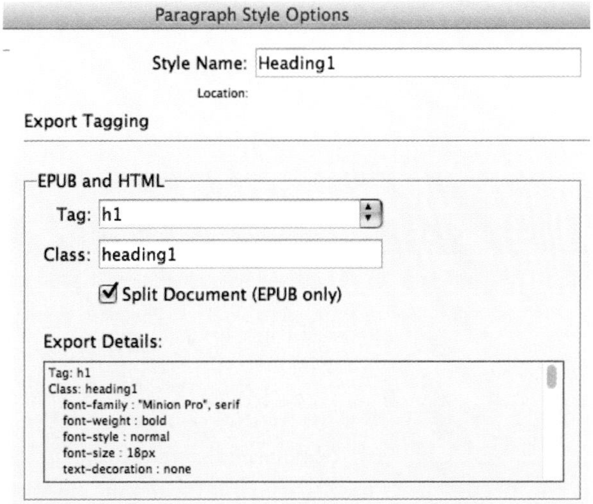

Paragraph Style Options

Style Name: Heading1

Location:

Export Tagging

EPUB and HTML

Tag: h1

Class: heading1

☑ Split Document (EPUB only)

Export Details:

```
Tag: h1
Class: heading1
    font-family : "Minion Pro", serif
    font-weight : bold
    font-style : normal
    font-size : 18px
    text-decoration : none
```

Mapping paragraph and character styles to HTML tags creates better code, making it easier to edit and more likely to be read correctly by ePub readers.

TIP You can edit the mapping of all your paragraph and character styles at once by choosing Edit All Export Tags from the Paragraph Styles panel menu.

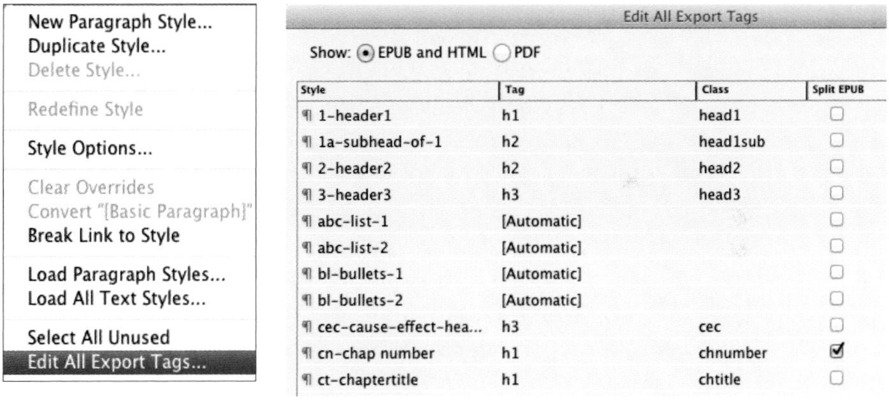

New Paragraph Style...
Duplicate Style...
Delete Style...

Redefine Style

Style Options...

Clear Overrides
Convert "[Basic Paragraph]"
Break Link to Style

Load Paragraph Styles...
Load All Text Styles...

Select All Unused
Edit All Export Tags...

Edit All Export Tags

Show: ● EPUB and HTML ○ PDF

| Style | Tag | Class | Split EPUB |
|---|---|---|---|
| ¶ 1-header1 | h1 | head1 | ☐ |
| ¶ 1a-subhead-of-1 | h2 | head1sub | ☐ |
| ¶ 2-header2 | h2 | head2 | ☐ |
| ¶ 3-header3 | h3 | head3 | ☐ |
| ¶ abc-list-1 | [Automatic] | | ☐ |
| ¶ abc-list-2 | [Automatic] | | ☐ |
| ¶ bl-bullets-1 | [Automatic] | | ☐ |
| ¶ bl-bullets-2 | [Automatic] | | ☐ |
| ¶ cec-cause-effect-hea... | h3 | cec | ☐ |
| ¶ cn-chap number | h1 | chnumber | ☑ |
| ¶ ct-chaptertitle | h1 | chtitle | ☐ |

Use the Edit All Export Tags dialog box to set tags and classes for all the paragraph styles in your document at once.

# Preparing Files: Managing Graphics

Exactly how a graphic will appear in an eBook very much depends on the device on which you're viewing it. eBook readers vary widely in their device resolution and size of display, and some may not display in color. The traditional Kindle with the E Ink display will show the graphic only in grayscale. Other readers, such as the Kindle Fire and the iPad, can display beautiful color at full resolution.

The good news is that you don't have to prepare your graphics differently for different devices. Instead, format your graphics for the highest-quality device and let the other readers display them as best they can.

As mentioned, you should usually place your graphics in the text stream. But the Articles panel won't let you place a graphic *within* a story. There are two methods to do so: create an inline graphic or anchor the graphic. To create an inline graphic, start by creating a paragraph style (we'll call it Inline Graphic). You'll usually set its leading to Auto so the paragraph will expand as the graphic is resized. Often you'll add centering, space before, and space after attributes.

Placing an inline graphic

Add a new paragraph where you'd like your graphic anchored, and style it with the Inline Graphic style. Copy your graphic to the clipboard, and then click to place the insertion point inside the paragraph. Paste. The graphic appears within the text flow. When you export your ePub file, the graphic will appear inline, with the text before and after. You can adjust the spacing before and after by modifying the Inline Graphic paragraph style.

The Inline Graphic paragraph style holding an imported image.

The alternative method, anchoring a graphic, is even easier. In fact, if you have a graphic that is already positioned in your layout, you don't even have to move it. This is also the method to use if you want text wrap around the graphic.

When viewed with frame edges turned on, every frame that is not inline or anchored has a little blue square (called an adornment) in the upper-right corner of the frame. To anchor a frame, drag that square to the location in the story where you'd like the frame to be anchored.

To anchor the graphic, drag the square to the location in the story where you want to anchor it (left). You can tell that a graphic has been anchored when it displays the anchor adornment. Choose View > Extras > Show Text Threads to display a line connecting the bounding box of the frame and its anchor location (right).

TIP If you have trouble moving the object anchor point to a specific position, view the text in the Story Editor. The anchored graphic is represented by an anchor icon, and you easily drag it to reposition it.

You can use the Object Export Options dialog box (discussed next) to set the alignment, space before and after, and other attributes of the anchored graphic.

Object Export Options dialog box: The EPUB and HTML tab of the Object Export Options dialog box lets you set custom rasterization options, alignment, and spacing for text and graphics; most of its settings are duplicated on the Images panel of the EPUB Export Options dialog box. The Export dialog box sets the default settings for all of the graphics in the ePub file. The Object Export Options dialog box lets you customize those settings for each graphic.

Here are a few reasons why you might need to customize the graphics settings:

- Some graphics may require custom alignment, spacing, or resolution.
- If you use text in a callout or a cover, you may want to rasterize it at a higher resolution for better appearance
- While InDesign recognizes much table and cell style formatting, tables that are too wide for eBook readers may work better if they are rasterized.

TIP The Object Export Options dialog box is non-modal. That means you can leave it open as you apply custom settings to images — a great timesaver!

Converting InDesign-created objects to images: Earlier in this chapter, we said that InDesign-created objects (lines, empty frames, and so on) are ignored during export to ePub. There are a couple of ways to overcome this limitation.

When you use the Articles panel to select the export order for page objects, any InDesign-created objects you include in an article will automatically be rasterized. They are turned into images at the default image resolution in the EPUB Export Options dialog box. If you group these objects before adding them to the Articles panel, they will be rasterized and included in the ePub as one object.

If you choose instead to anchor an InDesign-created object, you can use the Object Export Options dialog box to choose settings to rasterize the object.

Using the Float options to create text wrap: To wrap text around a graphic on the left or right, apply a custom Float Left or Float Right setting in the Object Export Options dialog box. The command places the graphic where you have anchored it and maintains the text wrap you have applied.

Start by selecting an anchored graphic. Use the Text Wrap panel to apply the Wrap Around Bounding Box setting, with an offset from the text. In the EPUB and HTML tab of the Object Export Options dialog box, select the Custom Layout check box and choose Float Right or Float Left from the menu on the right.

Other forms of art are more religious or tribal in nature. These include *chavittu nadakom* and *oppana* that combines dance, rhythmic hand clapping, and *ishal* vocalizations. *Margam Kali* is a traditional group dance form traceable back to 17th century, originally performed during Syrian Christian festivals. However, many of these art forms are largely performed for tourists or at youth festivals, and are not as popular among most Keralites. Contemporary art and performance styles including those employing mimicry and parody are more popular.

Kerala's music also has ancient roots. Carnatic music dominates Keralite traditional music. This

The Custom Layout option Float Right (top) creates a text wrap object in the ePub, as seen in Adobe Digital Editions (below).

# Managing Document Pages

All ePub files must have a navigational table of contents (TOC). Each eReader displays the TOC differently.

Each eBook reader displays the navigational TOC in a different way. Left: the iBooks application on an iPad. Right: the Adobe Digital Editions application.

In the iBooks application on an iPad, the TOC is displayed when you select the TOC icon at the top left of the page. In the Adobe Digital Editions application, the TOC is automatically displayed in the navigation pane on the left, although it can be turned off.

Creating a
navigational TOC

To create a navigational TOC, you need to create a TOC style. You can learn how to do this in the "Creating a Table of Contents (TOC)" section of Chapter 2.

When you export from InDesign, in the General panel of the EPUB Export Options dialog box, select the name of your TOC style from the TOC Style menu. If you have created a book file, the TOC style must be defined in the style source document (*see page 196*).

Many ePub files also include an internal TOC, which looks like the TOC in a printed book. In a printed book, it would include page references that tell you where a section or chapter begins. In an ePub file, this is not required, but it provides readers with another way to find content if the navigational TOC is not visible.

Because there are no fixed-size pages in an ePub file, the internal TOC will not contain page numbers; instead, it will have hyperlinks to sections or chapters. You create an internal TOC by placing the TOC you have created for your book onto a page of your document (*see Chapter 2*). If you include page numbers in your document, they will not be included in the ePub file, but hyperlinks will be created that lead to the referenced section or chapter.

TIP An internal TOC is not required in an ePub file. However, if you later convert your ePub into a Kindle file, an internal TOC *is* required.

Creating a cover

Every ePub file needs a cover. Whether potential customers are viewing your ePub in the iBookstore, the Amazon bookstore, or an eBook reader, you want them to see a good cover image.

TIP When you're designing a cover image, keep in mind that it's just a thumbnail. Avoid small type and images that can't be displayed well.

Whether an ePub file or a Kindle file, the cover image has to be a single flat image in a supported format, like JPEG or PNG. Generally, 600 pixels wide by 800 pixels tall are the recommended dimensions, at 72–300 ppi.

When you're exporting your ePub file, in the General panel of the EPUB Export Options dialog box you can choose between None, Rasterize First Page, or Select Image.

The **Rasterize First Page** option both creates a correctly sized cover image and displays the cover as the first page in the ePub file. If you have created your cover art from multiple objects, group them first. Then choose Object > Object Export Options. On the EPUB and HTML tab, select the Custom Rasterization check box. If the cover includes text, set the resolution to 300 ppi. Since you want this image on a separate page in the ePub, also select the Custom Layout check box and choose Alignment and Spacing from the menu, and select the Insert Page Break check box and choose After Image from the menu.

If you choose **Select Image**, you can navigate to a properly sized file in the correct file format, such as JPEG or PNG. In this case, the file doesn't have to be in your InDesign document, or even created in InDesign.

The Object Export Options dialog box allows you to convert an InDesign page into artwork that can be used as a cover page.

**Making page breaks**

Just because you have started a chapter or a book title on a new page of your InDesign layout doesn't mean that those page breaks will export as separate pages in your ePub file. Most likely, they won't. To create a page break that will display in an ePub reader, you need to break your document into separate HTML files. There are several ways to accomplish this. Creating paragraph style-based page breaks: You can use paragraph styles to create page or section breaks in the ePub file. You can select as many paragraph styles as you like to create new page or section breaks in an ePub file. You can do it for an individual paragraph style by choosing the style in the Paragraph Styles panel and selecting Style Options. In the Export Tagging panel, select the Split Document (EPUB only) check box. When you export, in the Advanced panel of the EPUB Export Options dialog box, choose Split Document > Based on Paragraph Style Export Tags.

TIP If you're selecting more than one style to apply a break to, choose Edit All Export Tags from the Paragraph Styles menu. This shows you a list of all the paragraph styles in the document. You can then select the Split EPUB check box beside each paragraph style for which the break should occur.

Use the Paragraph Style Options dialog box to specify that a paragraph style automatically start a new page wherever it occurs.

**Creating image-based breaks:** If you want all the images in your document to start on a new page (such as illustrations at the start of each chapter), select the Insert Page Break check box in the Image pane of the EPUB Export Options dialog box. Then choose Before Image, After Image, or Before and After Image from the menu.

If you want an single image to be on a separate page, select it and open the Object Export Options dialog box. Select the Custom Layout check box and choose Alignment and Spacing from the menu. Then select the Insert Page Break check box and choose Before Image, After Image, or Before and After Image from the menu.

**Working with book files:** Breaks work differently in book files, as you're about to learn. When you export an ePub from a book file, each chapter will automatically start on a new page by default.

Working with book files

When creating an ePub file from an InDesign document, you can either place your chapters in one document or organize your chapters in a *book* file. Create a book file by choosing File > New > Book. Use the + button at the bottom of the Book panel to add chapter files to your book. Place the chapters in the order you desire by dragging their names up or down in the book file list.

Click the column to the left of a file's name to make that file the *style source*. The style source is the file that contains the styles, swatches, TOC style, and other attributes that you want your chapters to share. You can synchronize your book's styles by deselecting all the chapter names (click in the gray area at the bottom of the panel) and choosing Synchronize Book. When the sync is finished, InDesign may display a message that the synchronization was successful and files may have changed. Save the individual files and choose Save Book from the Book panel menu.

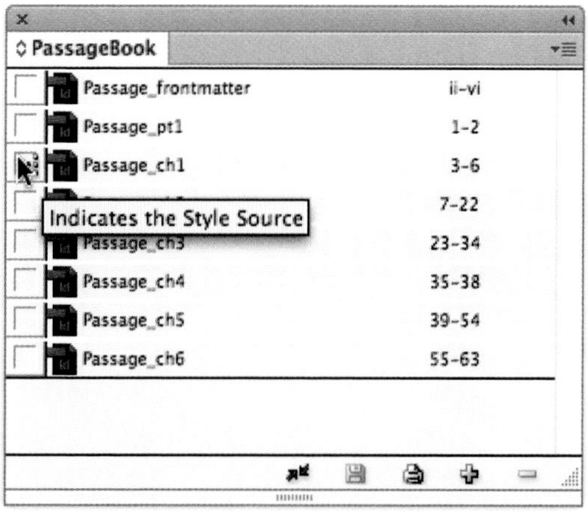

A book file can be used to number pages and coordinate the styles between documents. A book file can also be used to divide an ePub into separate sections.

---

TIP When using book files, you should place your TOC style and any metadata associated with the book in the style source document. Otherwise, it won't appear in the ePub file.

---

Adding metadata

It's important to include your book's metadata. Most eBook readers use information contained in the ePub file to display the book's title and author. You don't want the filename of the ePub to appear in a library as the book's title, which is what happens when there is no metadata. In some online eBook libraries, other metadata may be displayed as well.

To add metadata, choose File > File Info to open the File Information dialog box.

At minimum, enter the book title, the author, a description, keywords, and copyright information. We've experienced problems when the book title was missing from a document. But feel free to add other information as well.

In addition, two pieces of metadata should be added in the Advanced panel of the EPUB Export Options dialog box: Publisher and Unique ID. These are described in the next section.

The File Information dialog box lets you enter metadata for the ePub.

# Export Options for ePub

After doing the preparation work of specifying export order, styling, and other information, you're ready to look at a rough proof of your ePub. You choose the settings to accomplish this in the three panels of the EPUB Export Options dialog box.

General pane    The General pane allows you to set the ePub version and choose settings for the cover image, the TOC style, eBook reader margins, export order, and some text formatting options.

Version: There are three choices in the Version menu. The version of the ePub standard that is used by most ePub readers is **EPUB 2.0.1**. This is the version that was ratified in 2007 by the International Digital Publishing Forum (the IDPF is the organization that develops and maintains the standards for the ePub format). Usually, you'll choose EPUB 2.0.1.

A second standard, **EPUB 3.0**, was approved by the IDPF in 2011. ePub 3.0 adds extra features for including video and audio, exporting placed HTML and Adobe Edge HTML animations, and including external JavaScript. At the time of this writing, EPUB 3.0 is just starting to be adopted by ePub booksellers such as iBooks. You may have difficulty finding desktop software that supports EPUB 3.0 files. The third option, **EPUB 3.0 with Layout**, is an experimental format developed by Adobe Systems.

EPUB Export Options

General
Image
Advanced

**General**

Version: EPUB 2.0.1

(i) EPUB 2.0.1 is a standard approved by the IDPF in 2007. This format is supported on a wide variety of mobile devices, including smartphones, tablets, and eBook readers.

Setup

Cover: Rasterize First Page

TOC Style: [None]

Margins: 0    0

0    0    pixels

Content Order: Based on Page Layout

Text Options

☐ Place Footnote After Paragraph

☐ Remove Forced Line Breaks

Bullets: Map to Unordered Lists

Numbers: Map to Ordered Lists

☑ View EPUB after Exporting

Cancel    OK

The General pane of the EPUB Export Options dialog box is where you can set the ePub version and some text features.

Setup: If you have followed the workflow we described, the decisions about the Cover, TOC Style, and Content Order settings have already been addressed.

**Margins** refers to the space that appears at the edge of the reader window in the eReader. In many eReaders, this setting is not necessary, because the eReader provides its own margin around the page and ignores the Margin setting. In the eReaders that do not provide their own margins, such as Adobe Digital Editions, this setting specifies the margin on each side.

Text Options: The **Place Footnote After Paragraph** check box determines where footnotes in an ePub appear: If the check box is selected, footnotes display at the end of the paragraph in which they appear; if it is deselected, footnotes appear at the end of the current HTML file (the end of the chapter or the end of the ePub).

Select **Remove Forced Line Breaks** to remove all soft returns from the document. Each is converted to a single space.

In the **Bullets** menu, choosing the default option, **Map to Unordered Lists**, converts bullets created using InDesign's bulleted list feature into lists formatted with the HTML <ul> tag. Choose **Convert to Text** to format using the <p> tag, with bullet characters converted to text. This may work better when you're using custom glyphs.

The **Numbers** menu works similarly to InDesign's numbered list feature. **Map to Ordered List** is the default and converts to formatting with the HTML <ol> tag. **Map to Static Order List** creates list items using the <ol> tag but assigns a <value> attribute based on the paragraph's current number in InDesign. **Convert to Text** uses the <p> tag and converts the number into text.

View EPUB After Exporting: Selecting this check box launches the ePub reader for your hardware device so you can view a proof of the ePub file. This will usually be Adobe Digital Editions, if you have it installed.

Image pane   The Image pane controls the default settings for the ePub export of all of the graphics in the document. These settings can be overridden, graphic by graphic, by using the Object Export Options dialog box, as described in "Object Export Options dialog box" on page 191.

Preserve Appearance from Layout: This is a good default to leave selected. It preserves all transformations or effects you have applied to your graphic in InDesign. If you deselect this, the graphic appears in the ePub as if you had just placed the image fresh into InDesign.

Resolution (ppi): Choose an image resolution of 72, 96, 150, or 300 ppi for your graphics. 150 ppi is a good average choice.

Image Size: Specify whether images must remain fixed or will resize relative to the page. On some ePub readers, you change the width of the display window or change between portrait and landscape mode on the hardware device. If you choose **Relative to Page Size**, images rescale as the display changes.

Image Alignment and Spacing: These settings apply only to independent graphics, not to inline graphics. Whether they apply to anchored graphics depends on whether you select **Settings Apply to Anchored Objects**.

You can set the default alignment for images to left, centered, or right, and you can set the size (in pixels) of the space before and after an image. Select **Insert Page Break** to set a page break before, after, or before and after the image. (In the Object Export Options dialog box, you also have the option to float the graphics to the left or right of the text, which will preserve the text wrap attributes you've set in InDesign.)

Use the Image pane of the EPUB Export Options dialog box to choose default settings for the export of graphics in the document.

Image Conversion: Your choices are Automatic, GIF, JPEG, and PNG. If you choose **GIF**, you can select from the Palette menu. If you choose **JPEG**, you can select from the Image Quality and Format Method menus. InDesign's default is JPEG at the High setting, which is usually a good compromise between quality and file size. The JPEG format is a lossy format that compresses images to reduce the file size. The JPEG format supports millions of colors in the file. The GIF format is restricted to 256 colors.

The PNG format is a lossless format that supports transparency. Choosing PNG for all your images could make your ePub file very large. Ignore Object Export Options: If you have customized any of the settings for images in the Object Export Options dialog box, selecting this check box overrides those settings.

Advanced pane    The Advanced pane controls how a document is split (that is, how many HTML files will be created), what metadata is included, and some CSS and JavaScript options.

Split Document: The choices are **Do Not Split**, **Based on Paragraph Export Options**, or a single paragraph style. This menu is described in "Making page breaks," on page 195.

Use the Advanced pane of the EPUB Export Options dialog box to split a document, include metadata, and set CSS and JavaScript options.

EPUB Metadata: If you've followed the recommended workflow, much of the InDesign file's metadata has been included. In this section, you can also add publisher information and a unique ID, which will normally be the ISBN number of your book. If you don't have an ISBN, you can add any unique number, or InDesign will automatically generate a unique number (this is not the same as an ISBN number).

CSS Options: At the beginning of the chapter, you learned that an ePub file consists of HTML and CSS. InDesign CS6 will always generate its own CSS file to create formatting for the ePub. The choices you make here determine what InDesign will include in its CSS file. In addition, you can select one or more additional CSS files to specify the formatting. You might do this, for example, if you have a series of ePub files that will share formatting. After you have optimized the CSS code, you save it as an external file. You can then load this CSS for each ePub in the series.

TIP You may want to hire a CSS expert to define a custom CSS style sheet. A custom style sheet will give you maximum control over how the ePub file displays. Any custom attributes will override matching attributes in the InDesign-created CSS file.

Choose **Include Style Definitions** to write CSS for all InDesign styles that the user defines and applies. If you choose **Preserve Local Overrides**, any local attributes you've applied (such as italic or bold) will be included in the CSS. (But remember that using styles rather than local overrides creates cleaner, more editable code.)

If you choose **Include Embeddable Fonts**, InDesign will include encrypted fonts in the ePub file. It is quite likely, however, that they will not be usable on many ePub readers without additional tweaking. At this stage of the ePub standard, including fonts is a very complex issue. For more information on this issue, see this video overview "Embedding unencrypted fonts into an EPUB" (http://www.youtube.com/watch?v=_bWXfFsdSYw).

If you want to use one or more external CSS files, click the **Add Style Sheet** button, then navigate to the CSS file.

The JavaScript Options area works only with EPUB 3.0 files. Click **Add Script** to select one or more JavaScript files to use on export.

# Proofing and Validating ePubs

After changing the settings in the EPUB Export Options dialog box, click OK. If you have installed a default ePub reader, such as Adobe Digital Editions, you can begin the next step in the ePub workflow: proofing and validating your ePub file.

Proofing ePubs    To proof your ePub file, you should view it in one or more ePub readers. Initially, you may choose to view it in the free Adobe Digital Editions. It can be installed on both Mac and Windows computers. Download it from www.adobe.com/products/digitaleditions/.

It's best to proof in two or more programs, because they may display somewhat differently. Here are some commonly used ePub readers:

- **Calibre** is a multipurpose program that can be used for managing eBooks, reading ePubs, and converting eBooks to different formats (http://calibre-ebook.com/).
- **EPUBReader** is an add-on that allows you to view ePubs in the Firefox browser. Go to https://addons.mozilla.org and search for EPUBReader.
- **iBooks** is Apple's ePub reader app for the iPad and iPhone. Download it from the App Store. You can then install ePubs by opening

iTunes, choosing File > Add to Library, and selecting the ePub file. Open iBooks to read the ePub file.

■ **Ibis Reader** is a web-based reader you can use to view your ePub in a web browser. After creating an account, upload your ePub to your Ibis Reader library or just drag and drop an ePub to your browser (www.ibisreader.com/).

*Validating ePubs*

The EPUB 2.0.1 and 3.0 standards were developed and are maintained by the International Digital Publishing Forum (IDPF). These standards are sets of rules for how an ePub should be interpreted so it can be viewed consistently by different ePub readers. As of this writing, you'll need to validate for EPUB 2.0.1 because that's the standard that will be enforced if you want to upload your eBook to Apple's iBookstore or to the Amazon or Barnes & Noble bookstores.

The actual specifications are detailed on the IDPF website (http://idpf.org), but they are a bit complex to read and understand. The rules are also built into an open source application hosted by Google (http://code.google.com/p/epubcheck/), but you must be able to run Java from the command line and be familiar with command-line tools to use this tool effectively.

For the less technically inclined, a much easier way to validate files that are 10 MB or less is the IDPF's online ePub Validator (http://validator.idpf.org/). Just click Choose File, browse to select your ePub, and click Validate. If it passes, you'll get the message "Congratulations! No problems were found in *<name of ePub>*." If there are errors, they will be listed by file and line number in the code, which can help you identify the problem.

It's a good idea to validate your ePub after you export from InDesign but before you start monkeying with the HTML or CSS in a text editor. That way, you can fix any problems before you introduce new errors in your editing. For example, you might discover that some of the filenames of the graphics you've placed don't follow the ePub standard because they include spaces or special characters not allowed in the HTML.

# Going Under the Hood

Now it's time to get our hands a little dirty and go under the hood to view an ePub file. Inevitably, the ePub that is generated by InDesign will be lacking in some way, and you'll need to modify the CSS to fix a problem or enhance the file in a way that can't be done in InDesign.

*Cracking open the ePub*

The first step is to uncompress the ePub file, which is really just a special form of ZIP archive. This process is quite easy in Windows. On a Mac, it is a bit more challenging but can be accomplished with the right tools.

### In Windows

On a Windows computer, start by putting your ePub file into its own folder. (You do this because you'll end up with several files, which you don't want loose on your Desktop.) Then change the file extension from .epub to .zip, and extract the file using any ZIP archive utility.

After viewing or editing the resulting set of files (discussed in the next section), you can use the same utility to recompress the folder into a ZIP archive. Then change the extension back to .epub.

### On a Mac

On a Mac, the problem isn't in unzipping the archive, it's in correctly re-creating the ePub again after opening it. Because the Mac adds hidden data that makes the ePub invalid, you need to use a Mac-specific method. If you zipped the file, it wouldn't validate.

One method is to use the OS X Terminal commands to unzip and zip the ePub file. A much easier way is to use two free AppleScripts, EPUB UnZip and EPUB Zip. Anne-Marie Concepcion has described this method in a blog post (http://indesignsecrets.com/unzip-and-zip-epub-files-safely-with-these-applescripts.php). The method uses one script to unzip the ePub and a second to zip it again in a way that meets the ePub specification.

**Understanding ePub structure**

What do we see when we crack open the ePub? A structure of folders and files, including XML, HTML (or XHTML), and CSS files. You'll find the ePub's images in the Image folder.

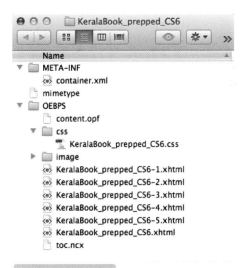

After unzipping the ePub file, you find a structure of folders and XML, HTML (or XHTML), and CSS files. Images are in the Image folder.

As mentioned at the beginning of the chapter, the ePub is like a mini website. Here's a short rundown on what the folders and files are used for, and whether you'd have any need to edit them.

META-INF folder: This usually contains only the *container.xml* file. It could also contain an *encryption.xml* file if you've embedded fonts. You won't need to edit the contents of this folder.

Mimetype: This is a single XML file that identifies the package as an ePub file. You won't edit this.

OEBPS folder: This acronym stands for Open eBook Publication Structure. This is where the good stuff lives. It contains the XHTML (or HTML) files that make up the text contents of the book: the CSS folder, which contains Cascading Style Sheets; the Image folder; and two XML files, *content.opf* and *toc.ncx*.

<chaptername>.xhtml: These files are like the body of the ePub file. They contain the structured XHTML code containing the content of your chapters or sections. You might edit these to change the content if necessary.

Image folder: This folder contains the optimized images exported by InDesign. You can view these in an image editor, such as Adobe Photoshop.

CSS folder: This folder contains the CSS files generated by InDesign as well as other CSS files you might have chosen to include when exporting the ePub. You'll edit these to change the formatting of your book.

TOC.ncx: This XML file is the navigational TOC that we described in the "Creating a navigational TOC" section on page 194. It displays in every ePub reader. Normally, you won't need to edit this.

Content.opf: This XML file could be considered the control center of the ePub file. It has three required parts and one optional part: The *metadata* contains information about your book, which we discussed in the section "Adding metadata" on page 197; behind the scenes, InDesign adds the required "date" attribute to this part. The *manifest* is a list of the files contained within the ePub. The *spine* lists the order in which the text files should appear in the eBook. The optional *guide* describes the role that each XHTML file plays in the eBook. For example, roles could include title page, dedication, and so on. Apple iBookstore requires this section for ePub files submitted to it. Kindle files require changes to the *guide* section.

Working with an ePub editor

To work with the files described in the previous section, you'll need to use an ePub editor. You could use any text editor, but it's better to use one specialized for working with code. (Don't use Microsoft Word, which saves files in a proprietary format. You want to save files in plain text format.) A good ePub editor will include the ability to search and replace code, will display tags with color coding, and will show the code in a structured way.

If you work with ePub files frequently, you may want to purchase a more powerful editor, like BBEdit for the Mac or Oxygen for Windows or Mac. These applications let you edit the ePub file without having to manually uncompress and recompress the file; the application takes care of that behind the scenes.

There are many ePub editors, and no agreement about which is best:

■ **TextWrangler** (Mac) is the free version of BBEdit. It supports soft wrap of lines, multifile search, and GREP pattern matching (www.barebones.com/products/textwrangler/).

TextWrangler for the Mac is an excellent ePub editor. Notice that it adds color to the HTML tags and indents the text to make it more readable. It also has panels that show open files and recent documents.

■ **Notepad++** is the Windows equivalent of TextWrangler. It's a free, open source application that has similar attributes (http://notepad-plus-plus.org/).

■ **Sigil** runs on Windows, OS X, and Linux. It's free, open source software that offers multiple views: Book view, Code view, and Split view (http://code.google.com/p/sigil/).

■ **Adobe Dreamweaver** (Mac and Windows) opens XML, HTML, and CSS files. It makes it easy to jump between related files. It has a Code view and a Split view, and it quickly previews in a browser (www.adobe.com/products/dreamweaver.html).

■ **Oxygen XML Author** (Mac and Windows) has all the characteristics of a good editor, but it also has some unique capabilities:

It can open an ePub file on the fly, make changes to any of its files, validate it, and then just as easily save it as an archive again (www.oxygenxml.com/xml_author.html).

While you may use your ePub editor to edit any of the component files of an ePub, the ones you're most likely to need to edit are the CSS files. We can cover only a few basics about Cascading Styles Sheets and give a few examples. We'll point to a couple of resources at the end of this section.

**CSS basics:** As an InDesign user, you have an advantage because you're already familiar with using styles.

In CSS, a *style* is a rule that describes how to format a particular piece of HTML. In the CSS generated by InDesign, this HTML is most commonly a paragraph <p> tag; a heading tag, like <h1>; or a <div> or <img> tag for a sidebar frame or graphic.

For a <p> or heading tag, you set properties such as color, font-family, font-style, font-weight, and so on. For a <div> tag, you set properties such as margin, padding, text-align, height, and so on.

**Types of styles:** A *tag style* applies globally to an individual tag that has a particular semantic meaning (like the top level, <h1>).

A *class style* is attached to text or a tag. A class helps to pinpoint to which elements the CSS is being applied to. A tag can be associated with several different classes, each applied to different elements. Class styles are most similar to InDesign's paragraph or character styles.

**The box model:** A web browser thinks of an <img> tag or a <div> tag as a box. To a browser, any tag is a box with something inside it — for example, an image or text.

Surrounding the content are the properties that make up the box:

- **Padding** is the space between the content and the content's border. The InDesign equivalent is inset spacing.
- **Border** is a line that's drawn around each edge of the box. This is like the stroke on a frame in InDesign.

TIP Unlike InDesign's stroke, you can choose on which sides the border will appear in CSS. If you select the top or bottom edge, you would create what InDesign calls a paragraph rule.

- **Background-color** is what InDesign would call the fill. It extends to the border.
- **Margin** is what separates a one tag from another. It's the space around the <img> or <div> tag. The closest InDesign equivalent is the space before or space after attribute.

Let's examine an example of how to edit the CSS. In the example book we're using, the print version was set up with sidebar frames that were placed away from the spine of the book.

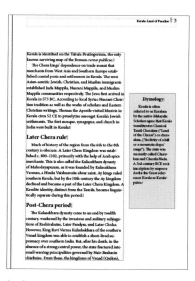

When the original print book was created, sidebar frames were anchored to the main text flow and an object style was applied to the frame.

When preparing the document for creating an ePub, we anchored the sidebar frame to the main text flow, as described in the "Anchoring a graphic in text" section on page 191. We then applied the Sidebar object style to the frame.

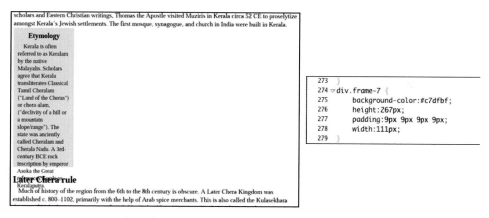

The frame dimensions from the book were preserved, but this no longer worked in our ePub document (left). InDesign exported the CSS for the Sidebar frame style (right).

When InDesign converted the document to ePub, it attempted to export as many attributes as possible. For the sidebar frame, it exported the `background color`, frame `height` and `width`, and inset spacing (`padding`).

However, because it included the frame's `height` and `width` properties, the sidebar doesn't display well in the ePub. It's too narrow and
overwrites some of the following tag.

This is a case where you need to edit the CSS. The box model doesn't
require including the `height` and `width` properties in the style. By removing these properties, the sidebar frame extends across the width of the
screen. In addition, adding a `margin` property for the frame added space
between it and the tags before and after.

in Kerala circa 52 CE to proselytize amongst Kerala's Jewish settlements. The first
mosque, synagogue, and church in India were built in Kerala.

**Etymology**

Kerala is often referred to as Keralam by the native Malayalis. Scholars agree that Kerala
transliterates Classical Tamil Cheralam ("Land of the Cheras") or chera-alam, ("declivity
of a hill or a mountain slope/range"). The state was anciently called Cheralam and Cherala
Nadu. A 3rd-century BCE rock inscription by emperor Asoka the Great references Kerala
as Keralaputra.

**Later Chera rule**

```
273    }
274  ▽ div.frame-7 {
275        background-color:#c7dfbf;
276        padding:9px 9px 9px 9px;
277        margin:9px 9px 9px 9px;
278    }
```

Removing the tag's `height` and `width` properties and adding a `margin` property improves
the appearance of the ePub.

Adding new properties
to the CSS

Because InDesign doesn't export all style attributes, sometimes you have
to add properties to the CSS with an ePub editor.

In the original print document, the Heading1 style included a paragraph
rule below the head. This is an attribute that InDesign doesn't export.

In the CSS, you can edit the `h1.heading1` style to add other properties.
To create a paragraph rule, you can add the `border-color`, `border-
style`, and `padding` properties, as well as individual `border-width`
properties for the four sides.

```
102        margin-left:0px;
103        margin-right:0px;
104        border-color: black;
105        border-style: solid;
106        border-top-width: 0px;
107        border-bottom-width: 1px;
108        border-left-width: 0px;
109        border-right-width: 0px;
110        padding: 2px;
111        text-align:left;
112        text-decoration:none;
113        text-indent:0px;
114    }
```

# Geography

Adding several properties to the `h1.heading1` style restored the paragraph rule.

**Learning more about CSS**

There are many sources of information to learn more about CSS. Elizabeth Castro has written several excellent books about creating eBooks. One of them — *EPUB Straight to the Point* — goes into great depth on CSS (www.elizabethcastro.com/epub).

**Converting to Kindle files**

Many of us wish that Amazon would adopt the EPUB standard, but so far they have insisted on staying with their Kindle file format. It was enhanced somewhat with the release of the Kindle Fire, but it still doesn't follow the EPUB specification. This means that if you want to offer your ePub on Amazon's Kindle Store, you'll need to convert your file to the Kindle format.

**Visit the Kindle Publishing Programs page:** Amazon provides a tremendous amount of information about creating Kindle files on their Kindle Publishing Programs page. There you can download the Kindle publishing guidelines and the applications mentioned below (www.amazon.com/gp/feature.html?docId=1000234621).

**Converting to Kindle:** There are three primary ways to create a Kindle file from an InDesign file. The easiest and most powerful way is to download and install Kindle Previewer, which you can use to preview and save the conversion from ePub to Kindle. The second method is to install the Kindle plug-in for InDesign. You then have a menu within InDesign that lets you save a MOBI file from InDesign (though it doesn't have quite as many options as InDesign's export controls). A third method is to download the free KindleGen application (available for Mac and Windows), which you can run from the command line to convert an ePub to a Kindle file. We don't use it, because we're not very adept at using command-line controls.

**Preparing your files:** The details for how to prepare your file and edit the ePub file's CSS are provided in the Kindle publishing guidelines, but here are the main points:

- It's a good idea to create separate InDesign and ePub files for converting to Kindle. That way, your ePub files can retain formatting that is not allowed in the Kindle.
- While Amazon recommends creating a separate 600 x 800 pixel JPEG image for the cover, if you use the Rasterize First Page method (*described in the "Creating a cover" section*), this image will work when converted with KindleGen or Kindle Previewer.
- You'll need both a navigational TOC and an internal TOC (without page numbers), as we describe in the "Creating a navigational TOC" section on page 194. The internal TOC should be the first text of the ePub file.
- Remove InDesign drop caps or they will be formatted badly on a Kindle.

Edit the ePub file: You'll need to make two edits in the ePub file with an ePub editor. First, open the CSS file created by InDesign (it's in the CSS folder). When you export the ePub file, InDesign writes an entry for Margin (in the Margins panel of the EPUB Export Options dialog box) even if you set the margins to 0 (zero). You must remove this entry from the CSS:

```
@page {
    margin : 0px 0px 0px 0px;
}
```

You must edit the Content.opf file to add a *guide* section. This appears after the *spine* section and will look similar to the example below. It must reference the image that InDesign generates for the cover and places in the Image folder. It must also reference the first HTML file in the ePub, which is where the internal TOC resides. You can see both of these references in the *manifest* section of the Content.opf file.

```
108        <itemref idref="KeralaBook_kindle_CS6-11"/>
109    </spine>
110 ▽  <guide>
111        <reference href="image/300.png" type="cover" title="Cover"/>
112        <reference href="KeralaBook_kindle_CS6-1.xhtml" type="toc" title="Table of Contents"/>
113    </guide>
114 </package>
115
```

Use Kindle Previewer: Open Kindle Previewer. Select the ePub file you specifically edited for Kindle conversion. Click OK, and Kindle Previewer will automatically open and convert the ePub file and then show it in the Previewer window. It will save the Kindle file in a new folder. From the Devices menu, choose among the Kindle, Kindle Fire, and other Kindles (including those running on an iPhone or iPad).

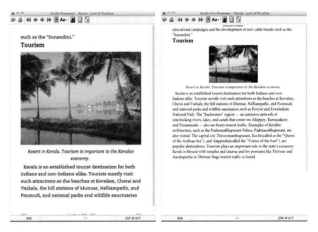

After converting the ePub file to Kindle format, Kindle Previewer allows you to select which Kindle device to preview it in. Shown are the E Ink Kindle (left) and the Kindle Fire (right).

# Evolving ePubs

The world of eBooks is changing and growing with great speed. What was true last week may have changed this week with new devices, evolving ePub standards, and even new forms of ePub files. Here's a glimpse of the changes coming to ePub files.

Changing standards

Since the ePub file format is controlled by the IDPF, their site is the best place to read about the EPUB 3.0 specification approved in 2011 (http://idpf.org/epub/30/spec/epub30-overview.html).

Switching to this new standard will probably be a slow process. There are already some EPUB 3.0 test files available, along with the beta versions of EpubCheck and ePub Validator. But the standard needs to be implemented on different ePub readers before you can use the new features.

Fixed-layout ePub

The EPUB 2.0.1 and 3.0 specifications are both for reflowable ePub, the kind described in this chapter. But there are books for which a reflowable format doesn't work such as children's books with lots of illustrations, or coffee table art books. These require eBooks in which the pages are static and objects have a fixed position.

To get around this limitation, individual ePub readers (including iBooks, Kobo, and Nook) have initiated the creation of what is being called a *fixed-layout ePub*. This is a fast-developing area. Check out Elizabeth Castro's eBook *Fixed Layout EPUBs for iPad and iPhone* (www.elizabethcastro.com/epub/).

Enhanced or multimedia ePub

When the IDPF was developing the EPUB 3.0 specification, some authors and vendors didn't want to wait to add multimedia (video and audio) and interactivity (using JavaScript). Apple took the lead by adding these capabilities to the iBooks application. Elizabeth Castro writes about this in the eBooks *Audio and Video in EPUB* and *Read Aloud EPUB for iBooks*.

# InDesign and HTML Export

Exporting InDesign files to ePub can be a pretty satisfying endeavor. With the right file preparation beforehand and some massaging afterward, the ePub export controls in InDesign produce a result that, well, looks like an ePub.

With HTML export, the result that most of us would like is a web page (or pages) that looks much like our print layout, with columns, colors, and images in at least roughly the same position. Unfortunately, this is not what happens, and if you're reading this section hoping to learn about one-click conversion from your print document to a web page, read no further. It simply doesn't exist.

InDesign's HTML export feature is not designed to give you instant web pages. It is designed to extract *content*, not page geometry.

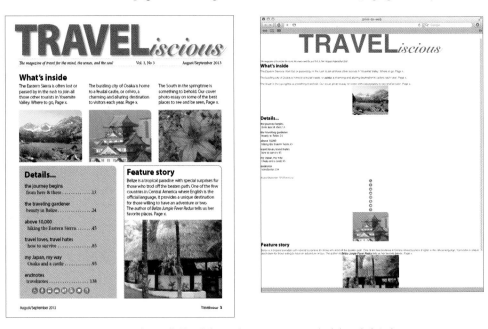

A print layout (left) and the resulting HTML export (right), with default export option settings.

But just because you can't create a finished web page, that doesn't mean HTML export from InDesign isn't useful. After all, moving the content from a print document to a web page is important, because so much information in print also appears on the web. And much of what we read in print today was created in InDesign.

How (and whether) you'll use InDesign's HTML export options really depends on your workflow and the skill level of your resources. You will almost never get a result that you can use on a website without extensive work on the code. So the question becomes, who will do the coding? Will you do it? Or are you part of a workgroup or organization that has designers to massage the basic files you provide?

TIP In order to export content from InDesign to HTML, you should have at least a basic understanding of CSS and HTML code, even if you are not coding the final website yourself.

# Preparing Files for HTML Export

If you plan to export your content to HTML, there are a few things you can do to prepare your InDesign document. They are similar, though not identical, to the steps required for ePub export.

First, if you are exporting your entire InDesign document, you need to establish the order in which the objects in your file will be exported. If your document consists of one long story thread, you will need to anchor all the images in position. If your document consists of many different stories and images, you'll probably want to use the Articles panel to order your document (*see "Preparing Files: Creating Reading Order," on page 183*).

One of the most important things you can do is use styles in your document. Paragraph and character styles are absolutely essential; object styles and table and cell styles can be helpful because they export code that can be used to format the HTML. It's also significant that InDesign allows you not only to style text, but to assign HTML tags to that text via the export tags that can be applied to paragraph and character styles. This helps form the content for use in a web page.

In organizations that have separate groups for print production and web production, simply adding export tags to existing InDesign styles is perhaps the single most useful thing a designer can do to create usable HTML code. The nice thing is that it does not burden the print designer with extra work, because once the tags are assigned to styles, the workflow for the designer is unchanged. For more information on using styles, see "Preparing Files: Using Styles," on page 186.

Images may need to be made part of the export order by anchoring them in text or by adding them to the Articles panel. In terms of optimizing them for use on a website, you can let InDesign convert them on export. However, most web designers strongly prefer to process images by using programs designed for the task of web optimization, such as Adobe Photoshop or Adobe Fireworks.

If you have just a few simple images or don't know how to use other programs to prepare images for the web, you can let InDesign convert the images for you. For more information on positioning graphics for export and using InDesign's image conversion, see "Preparing Files: Managing Graphics," on page 190.

# Export Options for HTML

Although ePub export and HTML export produce quite different results, their export options are nearly identical. This section discusses the few export options that are unique to HTML.

| HTML Export Option | Available in ePub Export Options |
|---|---|
| **General** | |
| Export: Selection/Document | No |
| Content Order: Page Layout/XML/Articles panel | Yes |
| Formatting Options: Bullets/Numbers | Yes |
| **Image** | |
| Copy Images: Optimized/Original/Link to Server Path | No |
| Preserve Appearance from Layout | Yes |
| Resolution (ppi) | Yes |
| Image Size: Fixed/Relative | Yes |
| Image Alignment and Spacing | Yes |
| Image Conversion: Automatic/GIF/JPEG/PNG | Yes |
| Ignore Object Export Settings | Yes |
| **Advanced** | |
| CSS Options: No CSS | No |
| Embed CSS: Include Style Definitions/Preserve Local Overrides | Yes |
| JavaScript Options | Yes |

General pane    The General pane of the HTML Export Options dialog box contains settings for choosing the export content and format options.

The General pane of the HTML Export Options dialog box.

The **Export** area allows you to export either a **Selection** of your InDesign document or the entire **Document**. To export a selection of your document, click the objects or frames you wish to export first, then choose Selection. This option is not available for ePub export; you can export only your entire document to ePub.

The **Content Order** options control the order in which the objects in your InDesign file or selection are exported to the HTML file. These are the same options that appear on the Content Order menu in the EPUB Export Options dialog box. **Based on Page Layout** will export objects in the order in which they appear in your layout, using the same top-down, left-to-right order used for ePub export. If your document uses XML markup, choose **Same as XML Structure**. You can also add objects to the Articles panel and use that for the export order by selecting **Same as Articles** panel. (*For more information on using the Articles panel, see the section "Articles panel" on page 184.*)

The **Formatting Options** area lets you control how bullet lists and number list will be formatted. These options work identically to those in the EPUB Export Options dialog box (*see the section "General pane" on page 198*).

Image pane     The Image pane controls are, for the most part, identical to the image export options for ePub.

The Image pane of the HTML Export Options dialog box.

The **Copy Images** menu options, however, are not available for ePub export, but they are very useful for workflows that include HTML export.

Choose **Original** to simply copy your original images into their own Images subfolder on export. The Images folder will be included in the *<document name>-web-resources* folder. You can then use a program such as Photoshop or Fireworks to optimize the images. When you choose this option, all other options in the dialog box are dimmed.

The Copy Images: Original option creates a folder that includes all the images in your InDesign document.

**Link to Server Path** lets you enter a local URL (such as "/images") that will appear in front of the image file in the exported HTML code, with the link attribute displaying the path and extension you specify. This makes it easy to keep your images in a subfolder and optimize them in a program such as Photoshop or Fireworks.

Link to Server Path lets you specify a path that will be written in the HTML code to point to your images.

If you choose **Optimized**, InDesign will optimize the images on export. All of the options in the dialog box become available, and they are identical to those for ePub export (*see the section "Image pane" on page 200*).

Advanced pane    The Advanced pane controls the settings related to the CSS code that will be generated on export. Again, the options found here are also found in the EPUB Export Options dialog box, with one important exception: By selecting **No CSS**, you specify that InDesign will not write any CSS code for you and that you will attach your own CSS file. For those who know HTML and CSS, this is a very good option, because a programmer can create much cleaner code than InDesign can.

The Advanced pane of the HTML Export Options dialog box.

If you want to instead include InDesign's CSS, choose **Embedded CSS**. You then have the options **Include Style Definitions** and **Preserve Local Overrides**. Click **Add Style Sheet** to link to an external CSS file. JavaScript can be added by clicking **Add Scrip**t under **JavaScript Options**. These options are the same as those for ePub export (*see "Advanced pane" on page 202*).

# Exporting PDF and SWF

# In This Chapter

THINK ABOUT HOW OFTEN YOU OPEN OR SEND A PDF FILE. It's such a simple idea: You create a document in one application and then convert it into a file format that can be opened by anyone using a free reader application.

As PDF technology has grown, it has been fascinating to watch how various groups use PDF files. Print houses use them as a prepress format. Editorial departments use them for marking up proofs of files. And publishers and design firms use the interactive features to create dynamic digital publications.

PDFs have been around a long time, and they're not considered terribly sexy anymore. But we've seen some incredible interactivity included within PDF documents. One author used PDF documents with embedded video files to create a college course on movie editing. A developer created an interactive Jeopardy-style game show with categories and questions in a table. Corporations have created annual reports with movie introductions featuring the company's CEO.

Like PDF, the SWF (Shockwave Flash) format can be used to create presentations and interactive documents. In fact, many of the SWF export controls are identical to the PDF controls. However, there are some important differences that you should understand before deciding which format to use.

# PDF Workflow

The InDesign workflow for creating and viewing PDF files.

It's simple to create a PDF file using InDesign. Once you create the file, just choose Adobe PDF (Interactive) and set the options in the dialog box. (*We cover setting the options for the document on page 226.*) Your readers then view the PDF file using a desktop application or a tablet app.

**Viewing PDF documents on Adobe readers**

Almost all of the interactive features in InDesign are usable in PDF documents. However, a few are not. The following table shows which features you can use in PDF documents when viewed on computers running Adobe Acrobat Pro or Adobe Reader or on tablets using Adobe Reader.

| InDesign Interactive Feature | Supported for Computers Running Adobe Reader or Acrobat Pro | Supported for Tablets and Smartphones Running Adobe Reader |
|---|---|---|
| Hyperlinks | Yes | Yes |
| Cross-References | Yes | Yes |
| Table of Contents | Yes | Yes |
| Bookmarks | Yes | Yes |
| Audio and Video Files | Yes | No |
| Multi-State Objects | No | No |
| Buttons | Yes | No |
| Forms | Yes | Yes |
| Animations | No. Animations must be exported as SWF files and then placed into the InDesign file as a movie to be exported as a PDF. | No. Animations are not supported, nor do SWF files play. |
| Page Transitions (*covered on page 247*) | Yes, except for the Page Turn and Page Curl effects. | No |

**Third-party PDF readers for computers**

In 2007, PDF became an *open source* standard. This means that companies other than Adobe can create and distribute their own versions of PDF creators and readers. They just have to follow the open source standards. They do not, however, have to follow the standards exactly.

This has been a mixed blessing. It has made it possible to download free or cheap PDF applications, but it also means that not every PDF reader supports all the features that are included in interactive PDF files. *And you won't know which reader your audience is using!*

For example, Macintosh computers come with a PDF reader application called Preview. Unless the Mac user downloads the Adobe Reader program and makes it the default application for PDF files, they will open your interactive PDF documents in Preview. Preview opens PDF files as "flat" documents. The image for a button, movie, or hyperlink may appear on the screen, but there will be no interactivity. The objects are still in the PDF, but they can't be used interactively.

Windows users may be using Adobe Reader or one of many third-party PDF readers. The problem with these third-party readers, such as the open source application Sumatra, is that they don't support any interactive features.

Your only solution is to firmly emphasize to those who open your PDF files that they should (*must!*) view it on Adobe Reader. You can send them to http://get.adobe.com/reader/ to download the software. The link looks at the computer's operating system and opens the correct download page. It's free, easy to install, and the most advanced reader for computers.

**Third-party PDF readers for tablets** It's really the wild, wild west if you're trying to find the best PDF reader for a tablet or smartphone. You would expect that Adobe Reader (from *Adobe!*) would be the best. Unfortunately, this is not the case.

At the time of this writing, Adobe Reader supports hyperlinks but ignores buttons. The third-party product GoodReader supports some button actions but not others. Adobe Reader supports bookmarks, but GoodReader doesn't. The best third-party tablet reader we've found so far is PDF Expert, but it costs $9.99 in the Apple App Store. You can't expect your readers to purchase a product in order to enjoy your document.

## Interactive PDF files on an iPad

The following is a good example of the adjustments you may have to make when designing interactive PDF documents for tablet devices.

Sandee created an interactive puzzle for *InDesign Magazine* by using the Show/Hide Button actions to display the answers to questions. When the first article was published, the editor got feedback from iPad users that the buttons didn't work. No wonder! The magazine had used the On Roll Over/On Roll Off button events to prompt the display. Roll over and roll off require a mouse!

So for the next issue, the magazine switched to the On Release or Tap event. Those button events do work on the iPad. Unfortunately, Adobe Reader for iPad doesn't support those button events.

The PDF reader that the magazine found that does recognize button actions is PDF Expert. But even then, the magazine had to convert all the text into outlines whenever text was used in a button or field. *InDesign Magazine* has to advise its readers that they may not get the puzzle's full, enhanced PDF experience when viewing the magazine on an iPad.

The only solution, at the present time, is to view PDF files on a computer running the official Adobe products.

# PDF Export

Once you've finished your InDesign document, it's time to export it as a PDF file. To do so, choose File > Export. You then have to choose between the Adobe PDF (Print) and Adobe PDF (Interactive) formats.

**Interactive or print?**  Why did Adobe separate the PDF export into two dialog boxes? Our best guess is that with only one export dialog box, users would inadvertently create PDF files for print that included interactive elements such as buttons and movies. Print prepress houses complained when they got PDF files filled with elements that screwed up their prepress workflow. By creating a separate export dialog box for interactive documents, Adobe avoids mixing interactive elements into a PDF designed for print.

The Export Adobe PDF dialog box for print (left) and the Export to Interactive PDF dialog box (right). Notice that there are seven sections for the print dialog box.

Here are the features and controls in each dialog box.

| Export Feature | Export Print Dialog Box | Export Interactive Dialog Box |
|---|---|---|
| Presets | Yes | No |
| Page Controls | Yes | Yes |
| View After Exporting | Yes | Yes |
| Embed Page Thumbnails | Yes | Yes |
| Optimize for Fast Web View | Yes | No |

| Export Feature | Export Print Dialog Box | Export Interactive Dialog Box |
|---|---|---|
| Create Tagged PDF | Yes | Yes |
| Presentation Controls | No | Yes |
| Create Acrobat Layers | Yes | Yes |
| Non-Printing Objects | Yes | No |
| Page Transitions | No | Yes |
| Export Layer Selections | Yes | No |
| Interactive Elements | Bookmarks and hyperlinks only | Yes, all |
| Compression | Full controls | Simple controls |
| Marks and Bleeds | Yes | No |
| Output | Yes | No |
| Advanced | Yes | No |
| Security | Yes | Yes |

We feel there are features in the print dialog box that would be helpful if added to the interactive settings.

- The **Export Layers** controls in the print dialog box allow you to choose which layers are included in the final PDF even if they are hidden or set to not print. The interactive controls export only the layers that are visible and set to print.

- Saving and applying **Presets** allows you to easily apply various controls to the dialog box. This is a real time-saver.

- The advanced **Compression** options in the print dialog box give you more control over how images are displayed in the PDF. The interactive dialog box has only simple controls.

**TIP** If you only need hyperlinks and bookmarks in your interactive document, you can use the export print dialog box. This gives you more compression options and allows you to use the saved presets.

**Targeting pages**     Most of the time you'll want to export all the pages in your document. In that case, just click the **All** selection.

Specifying pages and page ranges

If you want only certain pages to print, you can designate those pages in the **Range** field of the dialog box. Enter a comma to separate pages, such as 5, 7, 9. Use a hyphen to select a range of pages, such as 3–6. You can even mix hyphens and commas to select ranges and individual pages, such as 3, 5, 7–9.

### Specifying pages in sections

It gets a little complicated when you have alternate layouts in the document. Each alternate layout starts a new section and then restarts the page numbering. In that case, you can have two pages with the same page number. If you enter that page number in the dialog box, InDesign shows an alert that explains you need to be more specific.

To export a specific page, you can type the alternate layout name with a colon in front of the page number. For example, if you have an alternate layout called "iPad H," you would enter *iPad H:1* to export page 1 from that alternate layout. You can also type a plus sign (+) followed by the absolute page number in the document. So, for instance, if the page is the fourth actual page in the document, you would type +4 to export that page.

When you have alternate layouts in a document, you can insert the name of the alternate layout to specify which pages should be exported.

**Creating pages or spreads**

You can choose to export the PDF in single pages or to maintain the spreads in the document. For interactive documents, we usually deselect the spread option and break the document into single pages. This makes it easier to view all the information on the page without having to zoom in or out on a spread.

**Viewing after exporting**

The **View After Exporting** command may seem a trivial thing. But we firmly suggest turning this on, especially if you're going to be exporting and previewing your PDF over and over. You really want to immediately view the PDF without having to navigate to open it.

**Embedding page thumbnails**

The Embed Page Thumbnails option creates a thumbnail preview for each page being exported, or one thumbnail for each spread if the Spreads option is selected. These thumbnail images are then displayed in the PDF Pages pane as a preview of the document.

This option was important in the past, when it took longer to see the previews in the Pages pane. It is not as important now, when the page thumbnails are automatically created on the fly. We can't think of a situation where it is necessary.

**Creating Acrobat layers**

Select the option **Create Acrobat Layers** to convert the layers in the InDesign document into layers in the PDF file. This allows your viewers to show or hide layers using the Layers pane in Acrobat Pro or Adobe Reader.

However, instructing viewers where the Layers panel is and how to use it can be confusing. Fortunately, you can create buttons that will show or hide the layers in the document. Unfortunately, the Show Layers and Hide Layers actions are missing from InDesign's Buttons and Forms panel. You need to wait until you open the file in Acrobat Pro and then create the button action there.

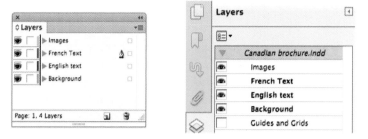
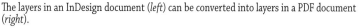

The layers in an InDesign document (*left*) can be converted into layers in a PDF document (*right*).

**Setting the View controls**

You can control the magnification for the PDF when it is first opened. This is very helpful if you want to ensure that the first page opens in the best magnification. Choose one of the following from the View menu:

- **Default** sets the magnification to whatever setting has been chosen on the viewer's machine. This can cause your document to open too large to be seen completely or too small to be read. Change this to have the document open to the setting you want.
- **Actual Size** sets the magnification to 100%.
- **Fit Page** forces the width and height of the page to fit within the document window. This allows the user to see the entire PDF page at once.
- **Fit Width** makes the width of the page fill the width of the document window. This setting is helpful for documents set in the landscape orientation.
- **Fit Height** makes the height of the page fill the height of the document window. This setting is helpful for documents set in the portrait orientation.
- **Fit Visible** displays the items on the page and tries to exclude whitespace in the margins. This is similar to the Fit Page setting except it zooms in a little closer on the active area of the page.
- **The percentage settings (25%, 50%, 75%, 100%)** let you specify the exact zoom level for a PDF.

**TIP** The View settings can be changed in Acrobat Pro and Adobe Reader.

**Setting the Layout controls**

You can also control how the pages appear within the document window. Choose one of the following from the Layout menu:

- **Default** sets the layout to whatever setting has been chosen on the viewer's machine.
- **Single Page** displays only one page in the document window. When you scroll up or down, the next page jumps into position.
- **Single Page Continuous** displays a single page in the document window, with the previous and next pages slightly visible. As you scroll, the previous pages disappear and new ones roll into view.
- **Two-Up (Facing)** displays a two-page spread in the document window.
- **Two-Up Continuous (Facing)** displays a continuous band of the two-page spreads in the document window. As you scroll, the previous spreads disappear and new ones appear in the display.
- **Two-Up (Cover Page)** is the same as Two-Up (Facing), but the first page is displayed alone. This is useful for any facing-page document with a cover page in the InDesign file.
- **Two-Up Continuous (Cover Page)** is the same as Two-Up Continuous (Facing), but the first page is displayed alone.

**TIP** The Layout settings can be modified in Acrobat Pro and Adobe Reader.

**Presentation controls**

You can set the PDF to open as a presentation. Select the **Open in Full Screen Mode** check box. This opens the PDF with a black background and no document window or screen controls. Instead of using Microsoft PowerPoint, you can convert your InDesign documents into PDF presentations. With a PDF, readers can use the left and right arrow keys to move from page to page. Press the ESC (escape) key to switch out of Full Screen mode.

Once you have set the document to open in Full Screen mode, you can select the Flip Pages Every *x* Seconds check box to automatically change pages every certain number of seconds.

You can also apply page transitions to the PDF document. Page transitions are covered on page 247, later in this chapter.

**TIP** The Presentation controls can be overridden by changing the settings in Acrobat Pro or Adobe Reader.

Presentation: ☑ Open in Full Screen Mode
☑ Flip Pages Every: 5    seconds
Page Transitions: | From Document    ⬍ |

The Presentation settings for opening the PDF in Full Screen mode and for moving from page to page.

## The Full Screen mode warning

It used to be that you could set a PDF to open in Full Screen mode and your viewers would be treated to a dark screen with your presentation ready to run. But then the security police made Adobe change things.

These days, a warning appears when a document starts to open in Full Screen mode. It warns users that "This document is trying to put Acrobat in full screen mode, which takes over your screen..." The alert goes on, but it is doubtful your readers will ever get to the end. Scared out of their wits, they will click the No button to close the dialog box and never open your PDF again.

This warning limits your use of Full Screen mode to only those people who understand the warning. There is a preference to disable the warning when you open PDF files, but only the person who opens the file can set it.

It's a shame, because it used to be fun to create PDF files that automatically opened as a presentation. We don't do it anymore.

**Including forms and media**

You can also choose the Forms and Media controls Include All or Appearance Only. **Include All** exports the document with the interactive objects.

**Appearance Only** omits exporting those objects and includes only the object's image. You may find this setting useful if you want a PDF developer to create the interactive forms and elements within Acrobat itself, which offers more advanced form field options, such as summing values or counting check boxes. This is a way to use the advanced appearances of InDesign objects with Acrobat's specialized buttons and form fields.

# Setting Accessibility Controls for PDF Files

You can't assume that the information on your pages is always consumed by sighted users. You should consider the needs of sight-impaired users who may be listening to the content of the PDF on a screen reader device.

You need to set the order in which the text and the descriptions of the images will be read. You also need to set the order in which the user will tab through forms and buttons on the page.

**TIP** You can listen to a PDF by opening it in Acrobat Pro or Adobe Reader and choosing View > Read Out Loud > Activate Read Out Loud. You can then select the commands to Read, Stop, and Pause the document. We use this to check that we've set the correct reading order of our documents.

## Section 508 accessibility

Setting the correct reading and tab order with descriptions is one of the accessibility settings for electronic documents that are required by government agencies under Section 508 of the Workforce Rehabilitation Act. Many countries outside the US have similar accessibility requirements for electronic documents.

If you do work for a department of the US government — or any part of your company works with the US government — you need to make your electronic documents accessible. In addition, companies may require that their documentation for human resources and other departments be accessible under the Americans With Disabilites Act. Aside from the laws, it's only polite to create the right tab order for sight-impaired users of your PDF documents.

**Applying descriptions**

Web page designers are familiar with the <alt> tag, which applies a description to visuals on the page. These alt tags are the text that is read aloud by screen readers. This is much more useful than listening to the drone of "image 1 JPEG, image 2 JPEG" and so on down the page. In a PDF, these are the **PDF descriptions,** or **alt text,** of the objects.

The descriptions for buttons and forms are placed in the PDF Options Description field in the Buttons and Forms panel. (*See Chapter 2, "Interactive Tools," for how to set these descriptions.*) You don't set descriptions for text frames. The text in the frame is the text that is read by the screen reader — from top to bottom.

But what about images? They have neither text nor description fields. What do you do for those objects?

The Object Export Options dialog box set to the Alt Text area. This is where you can enter the text for descriptions of placed graphics.

Choose Object > Object Export Options to open the Object Export Options dialog box. (This dialog box is also used to control objects for ePub export.) Click the **Alt Text** tab of the dialog box. Choose **Custom** from the **Alt Text Source** menu and then type the description in the field. You can type as much as you want to describe the image.

Setting the reading order

Without adjustments, the reading order for a page comes from the settings in Acrobat Pro or Adobe Reader. This can cause strange text flow. So what should you do if you want your items to be read in a specific order? That's where the Articles panel comes in.

An example of the default reading order for a page.

Using the Articles panel

Use the Articles panel to drag items into the order in which you want them to be read by screen readers. Open the Articles panel (Window > Articles). The panel contains instructions for how to add items. Select the objects on the page and drag them into the panel. The New Article dialog box appears. Name the article and make sure Include When Exporting is selected.

The New Article dialog box appears when you add items to the Articles panel.

If you add several items to the Articles panel at once, they appear in the order in which you created them on the page. Text frames are labeled with the first few words of their contents. Graphics are labeled with their image names. Buttons and forms are named with their names in the Buttons and Forms panel (this shows you the importance of creating clear names for buttons and forms — you won't know which object is which if you've kept the generic names).

The order in which objects appear in the panel is almost certainly not the order in which you want listeners to hear them. To put them in the desired order, simply drag each item to the correct position.

You may not want all items to be added to the Articles panel. For instance, if you have a label that explains that the user should click a button, the button itself may have a description that contains the same information. You don't want the screen reader to speak the same information twice, so don't drag that object into the panel.

---

**TIP** You can also use the XML structure pane of the document to set the reading order of PDF files. But the Articles panel was added to InDesign specifically for those who do not want to work with XML code.

---

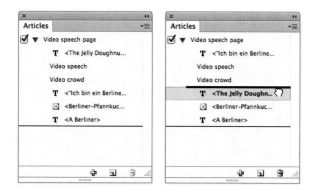

The Articles panel shows the order in which items will be read in the PDF. Drag the items to new positions to change their reading order.

Using the Articles panel, the reading order for the page is adjusted to make better sense. In addition, two objects on the page are omitted to skip redundant elements.

**Setting the tab order**

Reading aloud is just one part of accessibility. You also need to set the **tab order** for buttons and forms in your document. The tab order is the order in which the buttons and forms are chosen when the user taps the Tab or Shift-Tab keys. This is important not just for sight-impaired users but also for those "power users" who want to jump quickly from object to object. This is the order that puts the focus on interactive elements such as buttons and forms using the Tab key or Shift-Tab. The tab order comes from the order in which the objects are listed in the Articles panel.

**Setting the tagged PDF export options**

Once you have placed the items in the Articles panel, make sure that **Use For Reading Order in Tagged PDF** is selected in the Articles panel menu. This applies the order of the objects to the tab order in the PDF. Finally, when you export the document as an interactive PDF, make sure that the Create Tagged PDF check box and the Use Structure for Tab Order check box are selected.

Use the Tagged PDF options in the Export to Interactive PDF dialog box to set the correct reading and tab order.

# Image Handling

Most of the time, your InDesign files will contain images. You need to set the controls for how they are converted in the exported document. These settings are found in the Image Handling area of the Export to Interactive PDF dialog box.

The Image Handling area lets you control how images are converted in the exported PDF.

**Compression**

PDF files embed images within the file. This adds to the size of the file. **Compression** allow you to reduce the size of the PDF by ever-so-slightly changing the pixels within the images. There are three options in the Compression menu. The higher the compression, the smaller the final file size, but this has to be balanced with image quality.

- **JPEG (Lossy)** creates the smallest file size but can cause visible changes in images. If you choose JPEG (Lossy), you need to select an option from the JPEG Quality menu.
- **JPEG 2000 (Lossless)** compresses the images in the file without any visible changes.
- **Automatic** leaves it up to InDesign to choose the best output format for images.

JPEG quality

If you have chosen the JPEG (Lossy) option, you can choose an option from the JPEG Quality menu. Your choices range from **Minimum** (smallest file size) to **Maximum** (largest file size). Choose Maximum if you want your images to look their best. Choose Minimum if you don't mind some distortion in the image and want to reduce the file size.

Resolution

There are four options in the Resolution menu—72, 96, 144, and 300 pixels per inch (ppi)—but you can enter any number in the field. You only need to set a number higher than 96 ppi if you expect people to zoom in on your images. For instance, you might have a map that people will want to magnify. Setting a resolution of 144 ppi or 300 ppi ensures that there will still be details in the image at higher magnifications.

# Security

If you're going to send your precious PDF out into the world, you'll often need to control how people use the document. Can they print it? Can they edit it? Can they extract pages from it? This is when you need to set the security options. Click the **Security** button at the bottom of the Export to Interactive PDF dialog box. This opens the Security dialog box.

There are two parts to the Security settings: Document Open Password and Permissions. Each one is a totally separate security option.

Locking the document front door

You may want to specify that your PDF can be opened only by people who have permission to open the file. The **Document Open Password** area is the lock that keeps just anyone from opening the document. Only those with the password can open the file.

Select the option "Require a password to open the document" and then type the password in the field. You will need to type the password again to confirm you've typed it correctly. If you're going to send the PDF to someone in an email, send the password in a separate email. It's far less likely that both emails would be hijacked by people who you don't want to open the file.

---

**TIP** Make sure you write down the password or work on a copy of the file. We can't help you open the document if you forget the password.

---

Security

Encryption Level: High (128–bit AES) – Compatible with Acrobat 7 and Later

Document Open Password
☑ Require a password to open the document
　　Document Open Password: [＿＿＿＿＿＿＿＿＿＿]

The Document Open Password area sets the security to prevent the document from being opened without a password.

Permissions password

The **Permissions** password controls what people are allowed to do once they gain access to the document. What's confusing about this password is that it can be set without setting the Document Open password. This is the equivalent of leaving the front door open but locking certain rooms in the house.

**TIP** The Permissions password can't be the same as the password that opens the document.

Permissions
☑ Use a password to restrict printing, editing and other tasks
　　Permissions Password: [＿＿＿＿＿＿＿＿＿＿]

　　ⓘ　This password is required to open the document in PDF editing applications.

　　Printing Allowed: [ High Resolution ▼ ]
　　Changes Allowed: [ Any except extracting pages ▼ ]

☑ Enable copying of text, images and other content
☑ Enable text access of screen reader devices for the visually impaired
☑ Enable plaintext metadata

The Permissions password controls what actions someone can take once the document has been opened.

## Don't use these passwords

Information that was recently hacked from Yahoo! reveals the most commonly used passwords. The top three are *123456*, *password*, and *welcome*. These are pretty obvious and can be easily hacked. You should choose a password that is random, with upper- and lowercase letters as well as symbols such as #, >, &, or !. And the longer the better. An example is something such as *wgH$L8+dxew*. It's meaningless and long, and it contains a combination of letters, numbers, and symbols.

We also advise not distributing a PDF to the general public if you would lose your home, business, family, or reputation if someone were to hack into it. No security is 100 percent foolproof, and there are those who take it as a personal challenge to break into a password-protected file.

Once you have chosen to have a Permissions password, you have options as to what the person can do within the document.

### Printing Allowed controls

There are three options for how the document can be printed:

- **None** makes the option for printing unavailable.
- **Low Resolution (150 dpi)** limits printing of the document to only low-resolution printers. This keeps people from printing your document as part of professional output. Ordinarily, this would limit printing to only office printers, but there are some laser printers with resolutions higher than 150 dpi.
- **High Resolution** allows any type of printing to any device. We usually choose this setting.

You might want to limit printing to low resolution if you have images or illustrations that you don't want others using in their own documents. For instance, we've gotten a resort community PDF map that was set for low-resolution printing.

### Changes Allowed settings

There are five options for controlling what changes a user is allowed to apply to the document:

- **None** locks the document down, with no ability to change any items. This is the most secure setting.
- **Inserting, deleting, and rotating pages** allows someone to add new pages to the document, delete pages from the PDF, and rotate pages in the PDF. It basically allows page-level changes only.
- **Filling in form fields and signing** allows someone to enter information in form fields and use the digital signature to sign the document, but other changes are not allowed.
- **Commenting, filling in form fields, and signing** adds using the comment tools to the previous setting. Other changes are not allowed.
- **Any except extracting pages** allows anything within the document except sending pages to new documents.

### Allowed features

When you take away some features, you may want to re-enable others:

- **Enable copying of text, images, and other content** allows someone to highlight text or select an image and save it to another document. It also allows someone to use the Save As menu items to extract text, images, or both.
- **Enable text access of screen reader devices for the visually impaired** is automatically selected if the enable copying option is turned on. However, when enable copying is turned off, you have

the choice to turn this option on or off. Leave it on to keep your document in compliance with Section 508 (*covered on page 232*).

- **Enable plaintext metadata** encrypts the document but allows search engines to see the contents of the file.

# Setting the General SWF Options

**SWF** (pronounced swiff) is a format that, like PDF, can be used for the presentation of the entire InDesign file, with transitions from page to page.

In addition to the movies, sounds, and buttons found in PDF files, SWF files (commonly called Flash files) can contain the animations of page items from InDesign. (*See Chapter 3, "Animations," for how to create these motion graphics.*) SWF files cannot, however, contain PDF forms. As easy as it is to create these SWF animations and pages, you are somewhat limited as to where you can use them.

- The native animation effects won't play in exported PDF files.
- Apple doesn't support the SWF format for its iOS devices, such as the iPad and iPhone.
- As of August 2012, Adobe no longer makes the Flash Player that runs SWF files on Android devices.
- SWF animations need to be converted to HTML5 in order to be used in DPS apps.

Despite these limitations, there are still legitimate reasons to convert InDesign documents to SWF files.

- They are very easy to create, without the need to learn any code.
- They are great for web pages, adding small-file-size motion graphics.
- They create exciting presentations that can be played on a desktop computer or on a website. Diane worked with a client who created a private URL for a SWF presentation pitch to a client. The presentation used InDesign's animation effects with great success.
- They can be output from InDesign to SWF files, which can then be imported into an InDesign file (*covered on page 250*).

To export an InDesign document as a SWF file, choose File > Export and then choose the Flash Player (SWF) format; note that this is not the same as the Flash CS6 Professional (FLA) format (*covered on page 246*). The Export SWF dialog box appears.

The Export SWF dialog box.

**Controlling pages**   You can export all the pages in the document or just some of the pages. You also can choose the alternate pages for the file from the Range menu. These are the same options as for PDF documents (*see page 227*).

In addition to exporting pages, you can convert just the selected objects on a page into a SWF file by clicking the **Selection** button.

The Export SWF dialog box's Export controls for selections or pages.

**Generating an HTML file**   As mentioned, SWF files are great for web pages. However, in order to be seen within a computer's web browser, they need to be inserted into an HTML page. The **Generate HTML File** command creates a separate HTML file that contains the code necessary to insert the SWF into a web page.

The SWF and HTML files generated from the Export SWF dialog box.

**View after exporting**    Once you choose to generate the HTML file, you can then select the option **View SWF after Exporting**. You can't select that option without generating the HTML file. The HTML file will always be used to open the SWF in the default browser on your computer. (Your default browser is whatever browser you selected in your computer or browser settings.)

The browser must have the Flash Player extension installed to play the SWF file. If you have trouble playing SWF files, go to http://get.adobe.com/flashplayer/. That page will read your operating system and browser and display the correct download for your computer.

**TIP** The Flash Player extension is built into the Google Chrome browser for computers and is updated automatically when the browser is updated. That way, you don't have to update the Flash Player separately from the browser.

## The future of Flash

Flash isn't dead. There are still plenty of developers creating SWF animations, especially for gaming, but it does seem that HTML5 is rapidly taking over the space that SWF once occupied.

Although Android devices did support displaying SWF files, that support ended in August 2012. We wish there were a brighter future for Flash. But if we are eventually able to export InDesign's animations as HTML5 graphics, we will be happy.

**Viewing with Flash Player**    You don't have to view SWF content through your web browser. Go to www.adobe.com/support/flashplayer/downloads.html and download the standalone Flash Player application. This application lets you view a SWF file within its own window. Unfortunately, this application doesn't display page transitions.

**TIP** You can use the Flash Player application to create a self-contained SWF presentation (also called a projector) that doesn't require that Flash Player be on the user's computer. You need to create one project using Windows and another using the Mac. These files can then be distributed on a CD or DVD for presentations.

**Setting the size**    The **Size** area lets you change the dimensions of the SWF file. You can choose to scale the animation by a percentage, such as 200% or 50%, or you can use the **Fit To** menu to choose from some of the more common monitor dimensions, such as 1024 x 768 or 1280 x 800. You can also use the Width and Height controls to pick a specific size. Changing the dimensions of the SWF is very helpful when you need a presentation to fit precisely in a specific monitor resolution.

The Size controls let you change the dimensions of the SWF file.

**Background color**    The Background settings let you control what is behind the elements of the SWF file. **Paper** Color uses the color Paper from InDesign's settings. Use this setting when you want the animation to be easiest to read or to stand out from the browser. **Transparent** allows the color of the web page to show in the empty areas of the animation. Choose this when you want the animation to blend in to the rest of a web page.

**Including interactivity**    The Interactivity and Media setting is like the one for exporting a PDF. Select **Include All** to keep hyperlinks, buttons, and media active in the SWF. Choose **Appearance Only** to keep only the graphics for those items, without the interactivity.

# Setting the Advanced SWF Options

The Advanced tab of the Export SWF dialog box lets you control additional options, including timing, text conversion, image resolution and compression, and font embedding.

**TIP** As you move your cursor over the different controls in the dialog box, the Description field displays tips that help you apply the settings.

The Advanced tab of the Export SWF dialog box.

**Frames per second**

The **Frame Rate** field controls the smoothness of the animation. The higher the number, the more smoothly the animation will play. Changing the frame rate can be tricky to understand.

The Frame Rate field for setting the smoothness of the animation.

Let's say you have an object with a duration of 2 seconds moving onto a page at the default frame rate of 24 frames per second (fps). This creates an animation with 48 distinct steps. You see those steps as 46 green dots along the motion path. The start point is one step and the end point is another step for a total of 48 steps. If you increase the duration to 4 seconds, there will be 94 dots along the path plus the start and end points.

Duration 2 seconds at 48 steps

Duration I second at 24 steps

Duration ½ second at 12 steps

The green dots along the motion path indicate the number of steps for an animation. The higher the number of steps, the slower the object moves.

However, if you decrease the frame rate to 6 fps, the duration of the animation stays constant. The lower frame rate changes the smoothness of the motion. It's as if the number of green dots had been decreased to eight steps although you won't see any change in the number of dots displayed on the page. This creates an animation in which the object visibly jumps from one point to another along the path. (*See Chapter 3 for information on applying animations to objects.*)

Set the lowest frame rate that still makes your animation run smoothly. Some animations look good at 12 fps; others require 24 fps. Although raising the number may make the animation look smoother, it will also increase the size of the file. This can cause download speed issues if the file is viewed online.

**Handling text and fonts**  One of the reasons that SWF files became so popular on the web is that they keep the file size small by using vector objects in the animation (some people say that SWF stands for Small Web Files). Text is also kept as font (vector) information, which makes the file size small. However, there may be times when the font information doesn't translate correctly to the exported SWF. This causes certain characters to be dropped from the text or to be converted to glyphs.

The Text menu controls the treatment of text in the exported SWF.

In those situations, you need to change the Text setting in the Export SWF dialog box. Your choices are as follows:

- **Flash Classic Text** maintains the text as fonts, for the smallest file size. This is your best option for exporting a SWF.
- **Convert to Outlines** converts the fonts to their vector shapes. This option increases the file size.

■ **Convert to Pixels** changes the text to a bitmapped image, which results in a larger file. This option should only be used as a last resort, when converting to outlines doesn't work correctly.

When you maintain the text as Flash Classic text, you'll see a list of the fonts that have been embedded in the file. Most of the time, this will be a complete list of all the fonts in your document. However, some font publishers put code in their fonts that prevents them from being embedded in a file for export in a streaming animation. If that happens to your text, you need to change the font or convert it to pixels. Check the licenses of the fonts you are using for more information on what you can and cannot do with the font.

**TIP** Click the Font Licensing Info button to go to an Adobe web page that provides more information on font licensing.

Embedded Fonts (Applicable for Flash Classic Text only)

| Minion Pro Cond Italic Caption | ⟳ |
| **Myriad Pro Black Condensed** | ⟳ |

Font Name: Myriad Pro Black Condensed
Vendor ID: ADBE
© 1992, 1994, 1997, 2000, 2004 Adobe Systems Incorporated. All rights reserved. Protected by U.S. Patents D454,582.
http://www.adobe.com/type/legal.html

Total Fonts: 2          [ Font Licensing Info ]

The Embedded Fonts area for an exported SWF. Check this list to make sure that you haven't used a font that can't be embedded in the exported file.

**Rasterizing and flattening pages**

If you want a bitmapped picture of your animation that doesn't move, doesn't respond to mouse clicks, and basically just sits there like a bump on a log, select **Rasterize Pages**. The option removes all interactivity from your exported SWF. So why is it included?

Options: ☐ Rasterize Pages
☐ Flatten Transparency

The Rasterize Pages and Flatten Transparency options. These options should only be chosen for multi-page SWF presentations that can't be exported any other way.

Rasterize Pages should be used only for multi-page documents that are going to be presented using Flash Player. And even then, you should only apply the setting if you can't get the SWF to work correctly without the option applied. Basically, it's a last-resort measure to get the SWF to export. Because the option converts vector objects into bitmapped images, the option also increases the file size of the SWF.

The same warnings apply to the **Flatten Transparency** option. This setting removes all motion and interactivity from the document. It should be used only if the transparency effects, such as drop shadows or transparency PSD files, aren't exporting correctly in the SWF. It can't be used for motion animations, but it can be used for multi-page presentations.

> **TIP** A yellow alert symbol in the Export SWF dialog box indicates that the setting will remove all interactivity from the SWF.

Image handling
: The Image Handling options for exported SWF files are the same as the options for exporting images in a PDF. (*See page 235 for more information on image handling.*)

Previewing without exporting
: You may want to check the result of various options as you apply them in the Export SWF dialog box. If you export a file each time, you will constantly have to go through the steps to create a SWF, and you may also litter your desktop with files as you test the export settings.

Instead of creating extra files, you can use the SWF Preview panel to preview animations or presentations (*see page 85*). Choose Window > Interactive > SWF Preview to access the panel. In addition, you can change the export settings without actually exporting the document. You can edit the preview settings by choosing **Edit Preview Settings** from the SWF Preview panel menu. The Preview Settings dialog box contains the same settings as the Export SWF dialog box. Change the settings, and then use the SWF Preview panel to see how the file will export.

> **TIP** You can also choose Test in Browser from the SWF Preview panel menu. This opens your default browser and displays the animation without creating a file.

# Exporting FLA Files

There is one more option for working with animation files. Instead of exporting as a SWF that is ready to be placed into a web page or PDF, you can export the document as a native Flash (FLA) file. Choose File > Export > Flash CS6 Professional (FLA). The Export Flash CS6 Professional (FLA) dialog box appears.

Now before you get too excited about this option, be aware that the presets, timing, and actions for the animation are not imported as expected. Each spread is mapped to a new keyframe, and animations are visible in the Flash Library only as movie files that are set to loop continuously. This makes the file extremely complicated to edit.

The thought behind this export option is that you can send the native FLA file to a Flash developer, who can then integrate it into their own Flash project. We've been told, however, that the file is extremely primitive and hard to work with.

**Setting the FLA options**  Many of the options for exporting FLA files are the same as the options for exporting SWF files. The options for page ranges, size, including interactivity and media, and image handling are all the same.

The Text menu adds one option: Flash TLF Text. This lets the Flash developer use the **Text Layout Framework** options in Flash Professional. If Flash TLF Text is selected, select the Insert Discretionary Hyphenation Points check box to allow hyphenation of the text.

**TIP** Ask the Flash developer who will be using your file if they want these options chosen.

The Export Flash CS6 Professional (FLA) dialog box lets you convert your InDesign files into native Flash documents.

# Page Transitions

You have the choice to add transitions or effects that control how one page changes to another. You can set these transitions as you're working in the InDesign document or in the Export to Interactive PDF dialog box. These transitions are also used for the effects in multi-page SWF documents.

**Using the Page Transitions panel**  Use the Page Transitions panel (Window > Interactive > Page Transitions) to apply transitions to pages. Select the page or pages in the Pages panel and then choose the effect from the Transition menu. As you choose each one, the effect is displayed in the preview area.

Some of the transitions give you additional settings for the direction of the effect: down, left, left down, left up, right, right down, right up, and up.

**TIP** When you add transitions to pages, an icon appears next to the page in the Pages panel.

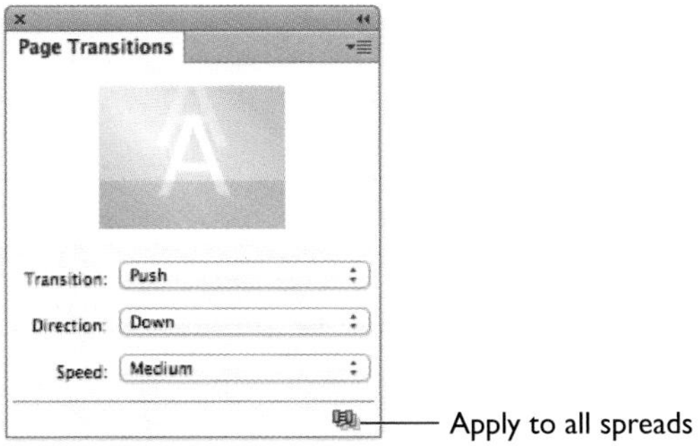

Apply to all spreads

The Page Transitions panel lets you preview and apply effects to page changes.

You can also apply transitions to pages by choosing Page Attributes > Page Transitions > Choose from the Pages panel menu. This opens the Page Transitions dialog box, where you can preview and apply all the transitions together. You can't, however, change the direction and speed controls of the transitions.

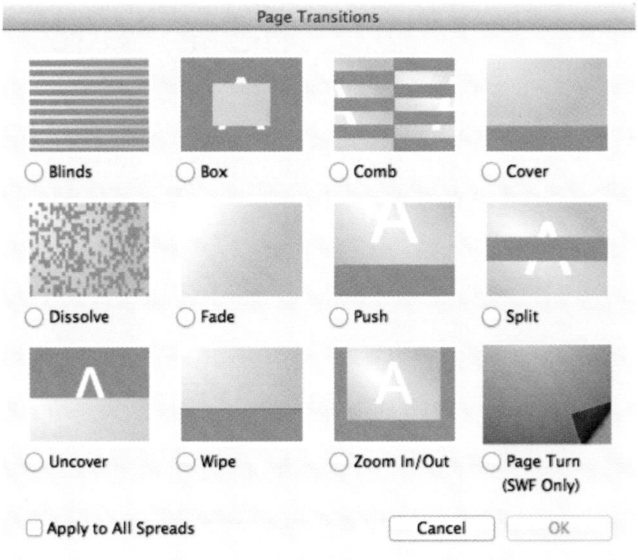

The Page Transitions dialog box lets you preview the animations for all the transitions together.

**Using the Export to Interactive PDF dialog box**

You can also use the Page Transitions menu in the Export to Interactive PDF dialog box. Choose **From Document** to maintain the settings applied in the file. Choose **None** to delete any settings. Choose one of the transitions to override the settings applied in the file.

**Previewing transitions on the page**

You don't have to wait until your file is exported to preview the transitions applied to pages. Open the SWF Preview panel and click the Set Preview Document Mode option. You can then click the forward and backward controls. The transitions are displayed in the preview panel as the pages change. (*For more information on using the SWF Preview panel, see Chapter 3.*)

Use the SWF Preview panel to see the transitions applied to pages.

**The page turn and the page curl**

There is a lot of confusion about the page turn and the page curl. These effects are *only available for SWF output*. They look alike but are invoked differently in the exported SWF.

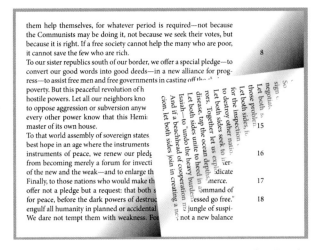

The Page Turn transition and the Page Curl interactive hotspot create the effect of a page flipping on the screen.

When you choose **Page Turn**, moving from one page to another displays the effect of a page being flipped over to the next. It's a very cool look and is duplicated in many electronic applications.

**Page Curl** can be applied to a document together with a page transition or alone as an option in the Export SW F dialog box. It creates interactive hotspot areas on the corners of the page that let the viewer pull the pages forward or back. It's a fun experience but can quickly lose its appeal.

The important thing to remember is that Page Turn is a transition that can be prompted with a button or click; Page Curl is a hotspot area that must be physically activated with a mouse.

# Exporting Animations into a PDF

An mentioned in Chapter 3, animations are supported only in exported SWF files. They don't work if the InDesign file is exported as a PDF. However, we do have some tricks that can help you display animations in PDF files.

Single pages

Our favorite thing to do with animations in interactive PDF files is to use them on a cover page. For example, picture an annual report whose front page has a brief animation that fades in to the image of the company headquarters. Since PDF files don't support animations, we need to make some adjustments to achieve this effect.

1. Start on the page that contains the animation. We like to put the page elements on their own layer.

2. Open the Export SWF dialog box and enter just that page in the Range field. Export with whatever settings you want for the SWF.

TIP Don't select just some elements on the page and export them. They won't interact correctly with other elements on the page.

3. Once the SWF has been exported, go back to the original page and hide the animation elements on that layer.

4. On a new layer, place the SWF as you would any image. You can now export the PDF with the animation on the page.

Multiple pages

You might also want the Page Turn transition to work in a PDF. In that case, export the entire PDF as a SWF with the transition applied. Then, delete all the information on the InDesign pages, leaving only a blank first page. Place the exported PDF on the page. You now have a SWF that contains the Page Turn transition to move from page to page.

SWFPresenter

We have come across a situation where someone needed each page of the SWF to be on its own corresponding InDesign page in order to use

Acrobat's timed slideshow feature. While it would be possible to export and place each page manually and then set the timing between each page in Acrobat, Martinho da Gloria of Automatication created a script, SWFPresenter, that automates the process.

SWFPresenter exports each page of your InDesign document to a SWF file and then places the SWF files on their own layer, making a tedious process easy. Once SWFPresenter has done its job, you just have to turn off the original design layers, export your InDesign document as an interactive PDF, and make the appropriate settings in Acrobat.

# B

# C

# F

# WATCH
# READ
# CREATE

Unlimited online access to all Peachpit, Adobe Press, Apple Training and New Riders videos and books, as well as content from other leading publishers including: O'Reilly Media, Focal Press, Sams, Que, Total Training, John Wiley & Sons, Course Technology PTR, Class on Demand, VTC and more.

No time commitment or contract required! Sign up for one month or a year.
All for $19.99 a month

## SIGN UP TODAY
**peachpit.com/creativeedge**